A KID CALLED EDDIE

CALLED

GROWING UP IN THE DEPRESSION AND WAR YEARS

Edward L. Wendland

LITTLE CREEK PRESS®
AND BOOK DESIGN
MINERAL POINT, WISCONSIN

Little Creek Press®
A Division of Kristin Mitchell Design, Inc.
5341 Sunny Ridge Road
Mineral Point, Wisconsin 53565

Edited by Grace A. Peters

Cover design: Jon Williquette

Interior book design and project coordination:
Little Creek Press®

Second Edition
September 2020

For more information or to order books:
visit www.littlecreekpress.com

Library of Congress Control Number: 2020913866

ISBN-13: 978-1-942586-84-5

Disclaimer: The following stories were written by Edward Wendland
as he remembered them from his childhood 80 years ago. Some minor
details may not be accurate, but he has penned them as accurately
as he can recall. All names in the book have been changed with
the exception of Eddie's parents and two grandfathers.

Dedicated to my mother, dad, and
Grandpa Phillips, who made these memories
of my growing up so special.

Table of Contents

Introduction

The stars above us glimmered, clear and shining.

Thousands of light years from the stars, my wife and I were the only ones on earth. Or at least that's how it felt. The damp air enveloped us in the darkness of the quiet night. Our children were in bed—all except the one still forming—and we lay on the grass in the front lawn, dreaming together and breathing in the silence.

We had three children and were expecting another baby in the fall. We started talking about the future because our house was far too small for four kids. We had looked for a home to buy and picked out one just a mile from my store. It was an all-brick house with four bedrooms, two baths, and a large living room and dining room. It was a luxury home, and we could well afford it on my pay.

But then I told my wife how much I liked growing up on a small farm. I wanted our kids to have the same life. Why didn't we buy a farm instead?

That night, I had a dream.

I dreamt I was a little boy, and I moved to a farm. It had apple trees, berries, and dozens of chickens of every color. I chased rabbits with my dog in huge woods that grew flowers and nuts.

I had a pet gander that loved me and followed me wherever I went. And my Grandpa Phillips played with me and told me funny stories and called me "Eddie."

Everyone gathered on Sunday for chicken dinner, and my parents loved me and cared for me.

It was a beautiful dream, and then I woke up and realized it wasn't a dream. ☆☆

Chapter One | 1933–1937
My Earliest Memories

Born in the Great Depression

I was born on August 28, 1933, right in the middle of the Great Depression. Pa said he was happy because when I was born, Prohibition ended. I really didn't think I did that myself. I had help from President Roosevelt. But either way, I'm happy today, and I drink my red wine.

Mom was sick after I was born and stayed in the hospital several months before she could come home. I was sent to stay with my Aunt Ella for almost four months until Mom was able to take care of me. A month after I was born, I was baptized as LeRoy Edward in Pa's Lutheran church, only to later find out that my birth certificate said my name was Edward LeRoy. Aunt Ella had registered me under the wrong name. Oh well! We all make mistakes. I like my name.

I was a small, chubby kid who seemed to always get into trouble. By the time I was three-and-a-half years old, whenever the family got together, the question was, "What did Eddie do now?"

Everyone in the family lived together. Most people couldn't afford to live alone, so they moved in with family. Sometimes we had as many as twelve people living with us, and I didn't even know some of them. Pa worked at Harley Davidson Motorcycle, but many men didn't have jobs. Prices were low because most people didn't have money. Bread was eight cents a loaf, milk was twelve cents a gallon, and we ate meat once a week. We paid $3.50 a month for our electricity and $8.00 a ton for coal. We could buy gasoline for eighteen cents a gallon, but we still didn't drive much. We rode the bus or streetcar for five cents and could go anywhere in the city.

These were hard times, but families were close, and everyone helped each other.

We lived on 56th Street, across from the Soldier's Home. Built after the Civil War, it was a hospital and retirement home for soldiers. It was located on a larger park off Greenfield Avenue. This was often the play area for all the kids in the neighborhood.

My Grandma Phillips had just passed away, and Grandpa Phillips had to clean out the homestead so he could sell it. All the aunts and uncles went over to help clean, and all of us cousins went to make a mess and play. The homestead was located on 11th Street across from South Division High School. Several of my aunts and uncles graduated from South Division, but my mom only went to eighth grade because she was the oldest and had to go to work to help support the family. Grandpa Phillips and Aunt Evelyn moved in with us on 56th Street. We had a large house with four bedrooms, and Mom wanted to take care of her little sister. Evelyn was not much older than my brother, Gene, and about ten years older than me.

My first memory was when I was three years old. Aunt Evelyn was trying to give me a haircut in the sunroom, and I was screaming my head off just because I was a pain in the rear. I would remain that way for the following fifteen years. She was more like a sister to me, but I sure didn't want her cutting my hair. We lived only four blocks from Greenfield Avenue, where we bought our groceries from a small store. Most families bought their groceries from small stores where they could get credit until payday. On Fridays, when Pa got paid, he would pay our bill for the week, and Gene and I would get free penny candy from the owner. Gene was going to school about five blocks from home. He was four years older than me and used me for a punching bag. That's what older brothers were supposed to do.

Three Strikes and You're Out

Today, if your kids are outside, you're supposed to know where they are every minute and what they're doing. Shame on my mother because I don't think she ever knew what I was doing. Usually, I was making trouble.

We had a very plain yard. The front of the house had several pine bushes, and the backyard had patchy grass and dirt. Everybody else in the neighborhood had pretty flower gardens with little figurines or dolls in bathtubs in their front yards. It was only fair in my three-and-a-half-year-old mind that some of those flowers would look nice in our yard. After all, I reasoned, the neighbors had a lot, and we didn't have any. So being the good boy that I was, I went down the street and pulled out some flowers to plant in our front yard. For some reason, the neighbors didn't want to share their flowers and chased me out of their yard. Then they had the nerve to call my mother. Mom was mad at me and made me go back to the neighbors and apologize for stealing their plants. Grandpa Phillips seemed to understand my logic, but you know how mothers can be.

Notice that the neighbors didn't necessarily say they wanted their figurines—only their flowers. So, being a good boy, I took my little red wagon the next day, went down the street, gathered a nice selection of animals and chickens made out of wood, put them in my wagon, and took them home for our front yard. I didn't take the doll in the one neighbor's bathtub. Later that day, the police came to our house and told Mom that I had taken all the lawn ornaments. Mom looked outside, and yes, I had taken them. We went back to the neighbors, but most of them were not happy. They told Mom to keep her little brat home. I didn't know what "brat" meant, but I didn't think it was a compliment from the tone of their voices. Strike one.

The next week, the neighbor girl and I decided to find some small stones and throw them at passing cars. We had little luck because her aim was no better than mine. So, we decided to walk down the street and throw rocks at the parked cars in the driveways. That way, we would never miss.

It worked! We didn't break any windows, but I noticed that we could get pit marks in the paint if we threw the rocks hard enough. No one stopped us, and when we got tired, we threw stones at a black and white car driving down our street.

Well, how were we to know it was a police car? Neither of us could read. The policeman made us get into his car, and we both started to cry. We weren't scared, but crying seemed like a good thing to do at the time. When we got to my house, Mom came to the door. The first thing the policeman said was, "Can't you keep this kid home?" Mom was really mad, but Grandpa Phillips was surprised that I had that good of an aim at three-and-a-half years old. He said that someday I would be a pitcher for the Milwaukee Brewers, a minor league ball team in the city.

Mom did not think it was funny. She had no sense of humor. Strike two.

Sometime later, I sat in my house on a beautiful spring morning and contemplated how to make Mom happy. Mom was still mad at me for bringing mice into the house, so I wanted to do something really nice for her. A few days before, the neighbor girl, Betty, and I had been playing across the road near the Wood Veterans Hospital fence. We tried to catch ants and put them in a cigar box. All we found were red ants. Since they bite, they're no fun.

We turned our attention to something else. It was our lucky day because we found a small nest of mice between the rocks. They were gray or brown with a lighter color on their faces and ears. I couldn't tell colors yet, but they sure were cute—something that Mom would love to have! We never had mice, just a big dog, and I was sure mice didn't eat much.

We caught them one at a time as they tried to escape and put them in our cigar box. Betty said she didn't want any even though we both caught them. We caught about seven little ones, but one jumped out of the cigar box and ran away. I couldn't wait to get home and give them to Mom. She'd be really happy with me.

We put a rubber band around the box, and I carried them home. Mom was scrubbing the floor on her hands and knees. I told her that I had gotten her a gift for Mother's Day, whatever that was. She took the rubber band off and opened the cigar box. She must have tipped the box because the mice dumped out and ran for cover.

Mom screamed. It didn't sound like a scream of joy. It took us over an hour to catch my little pets, and even then, one was missing. I was sent to my room (I seemed to spend a lot of time there). I could not understand why she was so mad. Grandpa Phillips thought they were cute, and they would make nice pets. He understood. Then Mom was mad at him for some reason.

After the incident, I determined on that beautiful spring day I would make it up to Mom. I decided to get her the prettiest flowers around—and not from the nasty neighbors. I knew there was a whole bunch in front of the hospital at the Soldier's Home, and those flowers were free.

Mom had just tied King, our German Shepherd, to the clothesline post. King didn't like it but was usually quiet until the school kids came by the house and taunted him or threw sticks at him. Then he would tug at the rope and bark and growl. King really didn't like those kids.

I tried to untie him so he could come along with me, but the knot was too tight. I took my trusty red wagon and headed across the street and through the fence to pick flowers at the Soldier's Home. I had been on the grounds many times with my brother, Gene, and the other kids. It was the neighborhood playground.

I followed the winding path past the cluster of trees and park benches to the main hospital located just off Greenfield Avenue, about five blocks from my house. The flowers were in full bloom in front of the hospital, ready for picking.

I picked a nice selection of colors and loaded them up in my wagon. Mom would love these flowers. Just as I was ready to leave, some lady dressed in white came running out of the hospital screaming at me. She told me to take the flowers out of the wagon or she would call the police. After all my work, this crabby lady wanted to steal my flowers! I dropped the flowers on the ground and headed back home without my gift for Mom.

I took a winding path through the grounds looking for something for my mom. By then, some of the old soldiers were walking along the path or sitting on benches. One soldier told me there were wildflowers along the cliff overlooking the valley. So, I took my wagon and headed for the valley.

In early spring, Menomonee Valley flooded easily. Sometimes homes and factories had to be vacated when the water got over three feet. By now, the flooding had gone down, and only small ponds of water were left.

When I reached the top of the slope, there was no path or way to get to the valley with my wagon. The old soldier was right. There were yellow, pink, and blue wildflowers that looked like violets along the top of the slope.

While I casually picked my flowers, at home, Mom noticed that I wasn't playing in the backyard. She went up and down the neighborhood calling for me. She asked some of the neighbors who were still talking to us if they had seen me. Of course, they hadn't because they still had their precious flowers and lawn ornaments.

Grandpa Phillips wasn't worried. He said they would soon find out where I was when the calls came in about my stealing something from yards. He was right. The police got a call from the Soldier's Home that a little fat boy (I resent that!) was stealing flowers from the hospital complex. The police sent out several squad cars in search of me. Mom and Grandpa Phillips called Betty's parents to see if she had gone with me. They said Betty couldn't play with me anymore because I wanted to play doctor. That was a lie because I never wanted to play doctor. Anyway, Betty was still home.

Grandpa Phillips and Mom joined the search, but I wasn't lost. I had filled my wagon with lovely wildflowers, talked to several soldiers seated on park benches overlooking the valley, and was now starting home. One of the soldiers gave me a piece of gum. I was told not to take anything from strangers (whoever *they* were), but no one said I couldn't take gum from a soldier.

As luck would have it (bad luck, I mean), the policeman who found me was the same one that I had hit with a rock. When he heard some fat kid (I still resent that) was stealing flowers and now was lost, he knew it was me. When he found me, he said someone should lock me up until I was twenty-one. He dumped out all my flowers in the shrubs, walked me to the car, threw the wagon in the trunk, and took me home.

By then, Mom and Grandpa Phillips had returned home and were waiting for me. When the policeman brought me in, he told Mom this was the last time he wanted to see me, and she should lock me up and throw away the key. Strike three.

After giving me hugs and kisses, Mom got really mad at me for getting lost in the Soldier's Home (I wasn't lost), taking gum or candy from strangers (it was just a soldier), and playing doctor with Betty (which I hadn't). Grandpa Phillips told me, "You can play doctor when you're older."

The next morning, Mom grabbed King's rope, and we walked out to the clothesline post. Then Mom took the rope and ran it through my belt loop and tied it to the post. King was let loose to run around, and I was tied to the post! Why isn't there a Humane Society for kids?

When the school kids came by and saw me tied to the clothes post, they did the same things to me that they always did to King. The moral of the story is "no good deed goes unpunished."

My First Swimming Lesson

One weekend in the summertime, the Phillips family—my mom's side—had their annual family reunion at Uncle John's cottage at Phantom Lake in Waukesha County. Uncle John had been out of work for some time during the Depression but rented this little cottage for quite cheap, so his family lived there for the summer and then moved to California when he was offered a job.

All the family was there. Many of the family came in from out of town, and I met them for the first time. It was late in the afternoon when Uncle John, Grandpa Phillips, and several others rented a boat and went fishing. Uncle John had a long pier on the lake, so Pa and the cousins fished off the pier. I was too young to even care, so I just ran around looking for something to get into.

As the afternoon got later, and the sun was going down, the boat came back from fishing. Grandpa Phillips's group had caught some large fish, and everybody gathered on the pier to see the catches. As more of the family crowded on the pier, I kept moving back so I wouldn't get stepped on or pushed off the pier. Someone backed up too far, and I fell off the pier, but no one noticed or cared with all the excitement and people. I might have been fat (chubby, perhaps), and I sank like a rock. I was only a foot away from the pier, but I didn't know enough to grab the post. Plus, I was drowning. Not much fun for a kid not quite four years old.

I had long, blonde hair, and finally, someone (I think it was Uncle George) grabbed me by my hair and pulled my head out of the water. Uncle Duke jumped in the water and lifted me onto the pier. I don't remember anyone else aware of what had happened.

Finally, Mom ran over and picked me up and carried me to shore. She asked if I was okay and told me to be more careful next time. I really didn't know how close I came to drowning, but I never wanted to do that again.

For several years after that, Mom, who was a great swimmer, tried to teach me how to swim. I would scream and cry and run to the shore. I don't think she understood how the pier incident affected me. Later, when I went to high school, we had to swim the length of the pool to graduate from gym. Somehow, I splashed my way from one end to the other and passed because I knew my coach would let me drown if I couldn't make it. There is a lesson here: never go to a family reunion on the lake unless you know how to swim.

Second Chance

I wasn't having a very nice summer. I was tied to a clothes post for two weeks, and I had almost drowned, and nobody cared. Everyone was mad at me, even Grandpa Phillips, my best friend. I always took Grandpa Phillips's tools and lost them outside. He wasn't very happy.

Mom was mad at me because of an incident with the dog. One day, King was hungry and there was no canned dog food for him. King only got one or two cans of dog food a month because we had to pay seven cents a can, which was too much to spend on a dog. We usually gave him the leftovers from dinner or bread and milk. I checked the icebox and found a package of raw meat that nobody was using. King was very happy with his meal, but Mom really screamed at me because there went our pork chops for supper.

Evelyn was mad at me because I cut my hair. She had made one of her nasty remarks to me while she tried to give me a haircut. I screamed and fought with her because she always scratched my head too hard with the comb. After she stormed off, I saved her the trouble and cut my hair. Then she got mad at me for helping her out.

Gene was mad at me because I gave his brand-new bag of marbles to Betty for her birthday. At least that day, I wasn't tied to the clothes post. I used to spend my time running around and around the post until I was tied up like the cowboys in western movies. I couldn't untie the knot, but I found that I could get loose if I slid the rope down my pants. My parents didn't know how to keep me tied up. That day I was free.

I sat in the backyard killing red ants with a flyswatter to pass the time. I never killed the black ants because Grandpa Phillips said they were the carpenters, and I knew carpenters built things, even if I couldn't see how those ants could build things. I didn't have any pets to play with since I had put my turtle in the toilet to swim. How did I know someone would flush the toilet, and he would stuff the drain? Pa was not happy when he had to take the toilet apart. I found out that turtles couldn't swim underwater for four hours.

First everyone was mad at me. Then something happened overnight. All of a sudden, everyone was nice to me again. When I woke up, Evelyn asked how the good boy was today. I didn't know who she was talking to. When I went downstairs for breakfast, Mom gave me a big hug and asked, "How is my very good boy today?" Everyone was treating me so nicely, but why?

I sat killing red ants and tried to figure out what was going on. I was usually greeted with a friendly, "You'd better stay out of trouble or else!" I had thought of running away from home when everyone was mad at me, but now everyone was nice to me, plus I wasn't allowed to cross a busy street by myself.

It was really hot, and I noticed that Betty's house had a sprinkler on in their front yard. Since Betty's parents had told me I was so nice to give her marbles for her birthday, I wanted to continue the friendly relationship. I took off my clothes and left them folded up on one of our lawn chairs and headed over to Betty's house. Pa said her family was rich because her dad owned a car business; that's why they could afford to have sprinklers in the front yard.

I ran across the street and started shouting over and over, "Betty! Betty! Oh, Betty!" Kids never rang doorbells or pounded on doors—that was for big people. We just shouted until our friends came out.

Betty's mother came to the door and took one look at me and asked why I wasn't tied up. "Get out of here and never come back!" she shouted. Betty was looking out of the window and waving at me, but her mother took a broom and said she would hit me if I didn't go home. The broom was a favorite weapon for parents. They never really hit anyone, but it was their biggest threat. Betty's mother threatened to call the police again, and I didn't want that. The policeman finally liked me because every time he drove by the house, I was tied up to the clothes post, and he would just smile and wave.

That was the last time I ever tried to play with Betty. Her mother called Mom and told her to keep her monster home or else. That was the end of being treated as a good boy.

Grandpa Phillips just laughed and said, "That-a-boy, Eddie. Strut your stuff." Whatever that meant. ⭐

Chapter Two | 1937
Moving to the Farm

The First Year on the Farm

We moved to the farm in September 1937. The farm belonged to Grandfather Wendland, but he was close to losing it to the bank, so Pa and Mom decided to buy it. Mom's dad and sister, Grandpa Phillips and Evelyn, came to live with us, too. I had just turned four years old, and it was the best day that I could remember. Pa unloaded the trailer with Grandpa Phillips, and Gene and I ran around the great new adventure. Grandfather Wendland was going to feed the chickens, so I followed him out to the chicken coop.

The chicken coop was an old vacated house built on the side of a hill. It had three rooms on the main level, and the lower level was divided into two rooms with windows facing the south. Grandfather Wendland had about twenty chickens in one room that was buried in straw and bird poop. It smelled terrible! The entry was small and may have once been a kitchen because it had old sinks and cupboards. He kept the chicken feed and extra straw in the cupboards. Old pictures were hanging on the wall, and everything was covered in dust and dirt. In the middle of the chicken house was a hallway with a stairway to the lower level. The coop had lights hanging from the ceiling, but they didn't seem to work. Many houses like this were vacant during the

Depression, but sometimes squatters moved in until the sheriff chased them out.

When we walked back to the house, Grandfather Wendland pointed out the grapevines, apple orchard, and berry patches. One side of the path had raspberries and currants, and the other side grew small produce.

Grandfather Wendland was over eighty years old, a tall, straight, handsome man. He used to be an officer in the German army and was very strict. When he came to America in the 1890s, he opened several tailor shops in Mankato, Minnesota. He retired at the age of fifty after one of his stores burned down. We always referred to him as Grandfather, never Grandpa. He was astute and aloof.

Mom and Evelyn were unloading boxes when we got back to the house, and Pa had gone back to the other house for another load. I went into the house, but I couldn't find the washroom. Mom said it was outside and walked me out to a little shed about fifty feet from the house. I had seen an outhouse before when we went fishing at the state parks, but I had never seen one by a house. My uncle Charles had one on the farm in Thiensville, but none of the outhouses I had seen were as dirty and covered with spider webs like the one at our new farm. Gene said he saw rats crawling out from under the outhouse, and I changed my mind about needing to use it and decided I wanted to go back home.

Mom told us that Pa would fix it up, and soon we would get indoor plumbing. It took eleven years for that to happen! Until then, we suffered with our walk to the outhouse at night and during the winter.

Grandpa Phillips loved the new house, especially the chickens. He worked in the coop every day, cleaning out the rooms and putting manure outside the door. I tried to help, but it was a stinky job.

When fall came, Pa couldn't afford to buy coal by the ton, so we would pick up twenty-pound bags at Wisconsin Ice and Coal in Milwaukee. It was owned by my cousin Carolyn's grandfather. By October, Mom and Evelyn were canning fruits and vegetables for the winter. We had a root cellar that was always cold and good for storing potatoes and onions and all the canned foods.

The house was very cold in the winter, and Pa realized that we couldn't keep it warm without burning coal or wood. He decided to cut down trees in the forest for wood. For the first several months, I wasn't allowed to go into the woods because I was likely to get lost. It was easy to find my way around the old house, but this was different. Gene was in school at the time so he could only help cut the trees on weekends. Gene hated living on the farm because he didn't like the hard work, cold house, and going outside to the outhouse (that made sense to me).

One Saturday, Pa and Grandpa Phillips loaded a two-man saw, buck saw, and ax into a small trailer and we headed to the south end of the woods. A dirt road ran from 87th Street to the old house, and it ended close to several dead trees. Pa chopped a groove into one of the trees, about sixteen inches high, and then chopped off the other side a few inches higher. He and Grandpa Phillips then used the two-man saw to cut through the tree. When it was ready to fall, Pa chased me over to stand by the chicken coop until the tree dropped exactly where he planned.

They cut off the branches with the buck saw and then the trunk with the two-man saw. Gene and I had to cut up the branches and carry them to the trailer. The men loaded up the logs and headed back to the house.

We worked over the weekend, cutting down trees and building up a log pile near the house. Gene had to take one day off from school to help with the large branches. For the next two weeks, the men split the logs, and Gene and I stacked them in the woodshed (garage) so they could dry out. We filled one side of the garage with logs and cut-up branches for the winter.

We had never had to do this in the city. Life wasn't easy in the country, especially when we didn't have money. Preparing for winter was a major concern that we weren't used to.

My first venture in the woods occurred when Gene and I went to pick hazelnuts. We filled burlap bags with clusters of nuts, stacked them in a coaster wagon, and stored them at home. Mom used the nuts for baking, and she shelled some nuts and salted them for munching.

Grandpa Phillips had a large winepress he had brought when he lived in Germany, so he busied himself picking grapes in bushel baskets and stacking them in the garage. Gene and I would put a bucket of grapes in the press, and Gene turned down the wheel on the press to get the juice. Grandpa Phillips put the juice in large barrels and added the sugar so it would ferment.

Grandpa Phillips also worked hard to fix the house windows (some were falling out) and repaired them as best he could.

Our House

The house was in bad shape. It was like stepping back to the turn of the century. We would have never bought the house except Grandfather Wendland was losing it to the bank. Grandfather Wendland was almost seventy-eight years old when he married Margaret Ronoff. Her family had owned this farm for many years since moving here from Pennsylvania. Before that, they owned a farm in Gettysburg during the Civil War. She claimed to have watched part of the battle from her second-floor window. The Union soldiers turned her house into their headquarters, and Margaret and her family were moved to an uncle's house in a nearby town.

Margaret and her family moved to Wisconsin in the 1870s and built the homestead on forty acres. She inherited the farm, but then almost lost it during the Depression. She ended up with one acre, and the balance was owned by the bank. There was a ten-acre forest behind the house and thirty acres of work land surrounding the house. The now-chicken coop was a second house on the property. When Margaret and Grandfather Wendland got married, they couldn't pay the bank for taxes. Pa didn't like his father because he had been cruel to his mother and hard on the rest of the family. But Grandfather was old and begged Pa to buy the property.

Mom and Pa's one advantage was that they could take the banknotes without money and pay the back taxes. Since they didn't have much cash, it was a way to own their first home. I don't think they realized what they had gotten into. The house was in terrible condition. The stucco was falling off, and the windows were barely holding in place. The furnace needed to be replaced, and the roof leaked. Every time it rained that fall, we had to put buckets in the attic to catch the water. The bank wouldn't lend us money to repair the house, so Mom went to work for several months to earn money for repairs. If we borrowed money, it was from loan sharks. They demanded high interest and required payment on time, or else you suffered the consequences.

The Farm and Surrounding Area

We were not fully prepared for the changes that would take place in our family when we moved from 56th Street. We moved from a nice four-bedroom house with two bathrooms and indoor plumbing to a broken-down house we froze in during the winter. Our old neighborhood was close to everything we needed, whereas the farmstead offered nothing nearby. We now lived on a working chicken and produce farm surrounded by a city. We were the last farm in the area. Gene went from a large, modern school to a rural school with a gravel playground. We didn't have a lot of money, but many of our new neighbors didn't even have jobs. Vacant houses surrounded us, and squatters lived in dugout basements or garages. Gene had just started going to Cub Scouts at his old school, and he had so many friends. Now, he found himself friendless at age eight with the stigma of being the only kid at school who lived on a farm.

At only four years old, I loved it. I could play in the woods every day, and I had chickens, ducks, and cats for pets. Most of all, I was rid of those nasty neighbors who had protected their precious lawn ornaments. Gene hated the farm and never got over it. He never played in the woods and never played with me. He had one close friend, and they both raised homing pigeons. He never wanted to go anywhere with the family, and when we went to a movie, he always sat by himself.

Grandpa Phillips was my best friend. I followed and worked with him all day and enjoyed the country life. Grandfather Wendland lived in an upstairs apartment with Margaret, and they were both nasty. He told me once not to come upstairs because he didn't like kids. That was okay with us because nobody liked him!

Mom and Pa worked very hard to rebuild the house and do all the outside work, but they never complained. In fact, Pa liked working with the chickens and the garden. We had great times on the farm and some awfully hard times, but we made it work.

Saturday Night Baths

Before we moved to the farm, we bathed several times a week. But on the farm, we could only bathe once a week, and sometimes, not even that often. We didn't have hot water and, of course, we didn't have a bathtub. Mom would have to heat large kettles of water on the stove. Mom filled a washtub in the kitchen for our baths, and Gene got his bath first. In the beginning, Mom filled the tub, and then Gene would wash himself since he was eight years old. But when the cold weather came, we couldn't keep the house warm, so everyone stayed in the kitchen at night where we burned a little wood stove. During the winter, Gene took his bath with Mom, Pa, Grandpa Phillips, Evelyn, and me in the room with him. Gene hated this and fought it every time. Since I was only four, it didn't bother me.

In the mornings, we helped take care of the chickens. Our coop was on the other side of the farm, and in the winter, the snow was deep. We all drank coffee, including me at four years old, because we needed something warm in the morning. At night, we had mint tea made from mint we cut on the farm. We seldom had store tea. Grandpa Phillips made his wine in the fall, and by December, we would start drinking it. Anytime we had a sneeze or cough, our parents would give us a glass of wine! Welcome to the country!

Rheumatic Fever

Our first winter in the farmhouse wasn't very nice. The wind blew through the windows, and the walls were freezing cold since the stucco was falling off the house. We didn't have indoor plumbing, so we had to take a flashlight and walk through the snow to the outhouse. At night, we kept a pail in the bedroom instead of going outside. The furnace didn't work well, and the house was very cold.

Pa bought a woodstove to warm the kitchen, and that's where the family spent their time. Grandpa would read or listen to the radio, Evelyn did her homework, Pa worked, and Mom played board games with Gene and me. We dressed in long underwear and sweatshirts when we went to bed. The room was so cold we could see our breath. I slept with a pillow on my head or wore a stocking cap because I got sinus headaches. We left a warm house for this?

One night, I was sitting on Grandpa Phillips's lap trying to learn my colors with little success (I am completely colorblind). I had a sore throat and chills. Whenever we got sick, we were given a small glass of wine, which cured everything from colds to warts. Mom rubbed my chest down with Vicks VapoRub (the seventh wonder of the world) and made up a cough syrup of honey, lemon, and onions.

By the next day, I had spiked a fever so high that Mom called the doctor, even though it cost five dollars for a house call. The doctor advised my parents to put me in cold water to get the fever down. A lot of kids in our area were getting fevers like this, but no one knew what it was. Mom got the kitchen stove full of wood to heat up the room and filled a washtub with cold water and ice chips from the icebox.

By that night, my fever was so high I became delirious and rolled out of bed. Pa put up the baby bed, so I couldn't roll out. After several days of the fever, Mom took me out of bed and held me on her favorite rocker. I was only four, but I could remember Mom rocking me in the chair and crying so hard that her tears fell on my face. The tears felt very cool. She prayed all that time, and for the first time, I got scared. I thought I was dying, and truly I came very close. It was the last thing I remembered from that night.

The next morning, I awoke wet from sweat. Mom opened her eyes, and I looked up and said, "Mom, I'm hungry!" The fever was gone. I was very weak after three days of the fever and not eating, but I was ready for food now!

I didn't return to my old self for a long time. I tired easily, lost my breath if I ran, and was pale. Mom took me back to the doctor because she was concerned over my constant tiredness.

After a number of tests, the doctor found that I had a heart condition I hadn't had before the fever. He instructed my parents to try to stop me from running or playing too hard and encourage me to sit and rest more. He thought it was something I would outgrow. We later found out he was not the sharpest doctor in town. He never even diagnosed my problem as rheumatic fever. Unfortunately, this was the beginning of a long-term problem.

First Spring

Although that first winter seemed to last forever, we made it through. We had used up all the firewood and drank all the wine, but spring had finally come. I was still weak and tired from my illness, but the April day when it hit seventy degrees, we knew we had survived.

Pa hired a farmer to plow up five acres for produce, and we all watched him walk behind his big workhorse and plow. Pa and I went to the local feed mill and picked up our first batch of chicks. Grandpa Phillips cleaned out one room in the coop for a hundred new babies and built a brooder with heating lamps to keep the chicks warm. Four large feeders and six waterers surrounded it.

The first batch of chicks were Leghorns (the best layers), and we eventually sorted out the young roosters for fryers. Within six weeks, we planned to move the chicks to another room and bring in a hundred White Rock or New Hampshire Red chicks. These were heavier birds, better for roasting, but still fairly good layers.

After the plowing was finished, we all worked to pick out stones and chop up clumps of dirt. Gene and I chopped with garden hoes while Pa and Grandpa Phillips pushed a five-pronged cultivator up and down the field. Our farm equipment included three garden hoes, two rakes, one push cultivator, and a wheelbarrow. It took us a week to break up the soil and start planting. Everything was done by hand. We planted ten rows of corn along the road and then potatoes, onions, peppers, and tomatoes. When summer came, the work would become harder. We planned to sell what we grew.

When we put in our seed, the ground was dry, and the soil didn't break up very well. Many of the seeds and small plants stuck in chunks of dirt. We finally got rain. It started to rain, and we all started to cheer. After three days of rain, we stopped cheering. We had so much rain that it saturated the soil and came through the stone basement wall until it flooded six inches deep. There was no way to pump it out, so we all filled buckets and carried them outside. Everything stored in the basement had to be moved upstairs to the kitchen to be sorted. The furnace didn't have a fire at that point, but the ash door filled with water. We didn't have a hot water heater or appliances, so there was no other damage.

The part of the seed that had been planted on a hillside washed away and was replaced by large gullies of water. Pa went out to see how the chickens were doing and found the brooder room full of water due to the roof leaking and the groundwater coming in. Many of the little chicks were floating all over the room. The lower level of the coop had standing water and the birds that were knocked off the roost drowned. After we moved the birds to a dry room, we gathered the floating chicks and put them in bushel baskets to carry outside. We lost a lot of birds and a quarter of our crops with that rain. Thank goodness all our berries did well.

Pa worked at Harley Davidson as a set-up man, and his plant was located at 38th and Juneau near the Menomonee Valley, the area where our old crabbing creek was. One area in the valley was called Piggsville. It was a small community located on the river and used by farmers to raise pigs for the nearby slaughterhouses. The homes there were completely underwater, and the village had to be vacated until it dried out. Once people returned, they would just have to leave again with the next flood.

Summertime and Better Times

When summer came, all the heartache and cares of the winter and spring were forgotten. By the end of May, we had some small produce to sell, but we didn't know where to sell it. Pa parked his car on vacant lots in town, but few people came for radishes, onions, and leaf lettuce. He decided to sell it door to door in West Allis. Each one of us carried a basket of produce and knocked on doors. Pa and I sold on one side, and Gene was old enough to sell across the street. We made little money, but it seemed to be the best method. Later, we sold squash, pickles, and cucumbers, and business picked up. I learned to count change by the age of almost five years old. When the raspberries came in, and some of the chickens started to lay eggs, we sold out nearly every day. Many of the customers took our name and location and started to place orders with us.

Every day, a dozen people came to our farm for berries, eggs, and produce. We started making enough extra money that we often went to the movies and bought popcorn and candy. I liked making money. Pa would pay us two cents a quart to pick currants and three cents a quart to pick raspberries. I hated picking strawberries because I was short and couldn't help stepping on the vines. Then I always got yelled at. "Eddie! Don't step on the vines!" Gene was older and he could quickly pick raspberries and strawberries, so he made good money. I was not quite five and was much slower, but I made six to eight cents a day—not bad for a day's work!

Although we lived on a farm, it was within city limits of West Allis. The ice cream man came around the block three times a week with his pushcart, and we could buy ice cream for a nickel. What a great life we had.

Charlie Lives

Charlie was as much a member of the family as anyone else. His skinny frame and broken wing made him the ugliest Leghorn rooster you've ever seen, but everyone loved Charlie. He practically ran the farm.

In fall, after all the crops were picked, we cleaned out our chicken flock. Every spring we bought several hundred baby chicks. Then we sorted all the roosters and moved them to a separate room to fatten up for the fall.

On three Saturdays in the fall, we butchered and sold the fryers and roasting birds. We had a chopping block, hatchet, stove, and washtubs in the basement for the process. Grandpa Phillips did all the butchering the first two years and did a great job. Sometimes we would catch wild pigeons where they roosted, and Grandpa Phillips could ring their necks in seconds. He was very good.

When Pa took over the butchering days, he couldn't kill pigeons and did a poor job killing the chickens. He never looked at the chicken when he chopped its heads off and often missed its neck, cutting off its wings. He actually cut the leg off one poor bird.

Everyone had a part in the chicken-killing process. Grandpa Phillips selected ten to fifteen roosters to be butchered. Pa butchered the birds, and Mom dipped them in boiling water and took off their outer feathers. Then she gutted each bird and handed it to Gene and me to take off the pin feathers. Each bird was numbered and put in the icebox until a customer picked up his order.

After we finished the butchering, Gene and I had to clean the basement. The floor was always covered with chicken heads, feathers, and blood. We had to pick up the mess, scrub the floor, and bury the chicken remnants in the field. It took four or five hours to butcher the birds and then clean up the basement. Gene and I hated the job, but we got paid twenty-five cents to do the daily chores and clean the basement.

Charlie was one of the first birds Pa was supposed to kill. As usual, Pa never looked at the chicken. He raised the ax, turned his head, and swung. He chopped off the tip of Charlie's wing. "Pa, please look at what you're doing," Mom said. Again, Pa lifted the ax and swung, but Charlie turned his head, and Pa missed him completely. Mom was getting impatient. Pa took another swing and got the other wing.

The rooster broke loose and started running around the basement with two clipped wings. It took us several minutes to catch him, but we finally gave him back to Pa. Charlie didn't seem to care about this process and wanted out. We all felt a little guilty when Pa grabbed him like he was really mad. Pa walked up the basement stairs with the chicken and threw him out the back. He hollered, "Goodbye, Charlie!"

Charlie lived in luxury for several years after.

A Day at a Real Farm

The fishing poles were tied to the top of the Ford, and our lunch and blanket were in the trunk. On this day, we were going to the Schmidt Farm. Aunt Dottie, Pa's older sister, lived on a dairy farm in Fredonia. We usually went there three times a year. In spring, we went to pick mushrooms from their woods. We always came away with large baskets of mushrooms. Mom would check each basket to be sure we hadn't picked any poisonous ones. I was told that a mobster named John Dillinger from Chicago used to hide out in those very woods surrounding Aunt Dottie's farm, but that was back in the 1920s.

In the summer, we always planned a fishing day on the Milwaukee River, and we always caught lots of fish. Then once a year at least, all the Wendlands would get together for a reunion or sometimes a wedding, always held on the farm. All my cousins were much older than me, and three of them had already gotten married.

We left our house at six in the morning and drove through what we called "the village" (Wauwatosa) to 76th Street and Grafton. Seventy-Sixth Street, or Highway 181, went by miles of mink farms. From the road, we could see the large sheds with outside cages attached. Mink fur, used for mink coats and fur pieces, was very expensive.

We followed the Milwaukee River to Highway 57 and on to Fredonia. Finally, we reached the large hill that went down to Aunt Dottie's farm and the river. When we arrived, Uncle Charles was coming from the barn with a pail of milk. He always seemed like a tough man with a very loud voice, like he was always mad. He used to make fun of chicken farmers.

The driveway was full of hay racks, large discs, and other equipment and junk. We couldn't find a place to park. They had a small, unpainted barn and an outhouse that looked even worse. We never used it if we could help it because Mom said they used the Sears catalog pages instead of toilet paper.

Aunt Dottie and my cousin Ruthie greeted us at the door. The house seemed small from the outside, but it had a large kitchen, dining room, and living room. The entry was full of barn boots and clothing that reeked of cow manure. As we walked into the kitchen, we saw strips of flypaper hung all over the rooms with dead insects stuck to them. But these could not accommodate all the flies still buzzing around.

Aunt Dottie was busy baking her morning bread on a wood cooking stove with an oven, like one I had seen in my old history book. She was so excited to see us because now she could show off their new electric lights. It was the first time they had ever had electric lights. Each room had a light and string hanging from the ceiling. She pulled the string over and over to show us their new addition.

When her excitement had worn out over the lights, we all sat down to have her famous apple strudel and a cup of coffee.

We drove down along the cow path to the river and our favorite spot. I loved to fish with Mom and Pa, but Gene took off with Tom, Richie, or another one of the dozen cousins. We had a great time, as we always did. The water was so clear we could see the fish chasing the bait. Before we threw the line into the water, we wriggled the worm onto the bait and spat onto the hook. Grandpa Phillips always said, "If you don't spit on the hook, the fish won't bite," and he was always right.

We caught so many fish we didn't have enough pails to put them in. Gene came back for lunch and then took off again with Ruthie and Richie. We always enjoyed visiting with Aunt Dottie because she was always so cheerful. We invited their family to visit, but they never came. Uncle Charles didn't like the smell of "them damn chickens."

Chicken Killer

Clear, crisp fall Saturdays offered themselves as perfect days to ride my tricycle horse on the narrow sidewalk next to the house. The tricycle had been bought at the 1933 World Fair in Chicago. I had always loved the horse, and I rode it all day long on 56th

Street, where we lived on a corner and had a sidewalk to ride on.

Grandpa Phillips was cleaning out the chicken coop, and King was running around the farm looking for something to play with. He was a big German Shepherd and required a lot of food. He lived off table scraps and bones, but sometimes there wasn't much for him to eat, and he was very lean.

King no longer had to be tied to the clothesline post. He didn't miss it, and neither did I. So, he ran around the farm all day.

Suddenly, Pa came running out of the house, screaming, "King! Drop that chicken! Drop that chicken!" One of the hens had gotten out of the coop while Grandpa Phillips cleaned. King chased her down, grabbed her by the neck, and carried her off. By the time King released the bird, she was half dead. He dropped the hen and knew he had done wrong. Hanging his head, he tried to rub up against Pa's leg to make amends. Pa angrily grabbed King by the collar and dragged him back to the house.

Grandpa came from the coop, and Pa explained what King had done. He wanted him to stay tied to the clothes post until he could be trained better. King was a good dog and should have had a second chance. After all, farm life was all new to a city dog. Grandpa disagreed with Pa immediately. "Once a dog kills a chicken, it's in his blood." King was now a chicken killer. He had killed a laying hen, and we would lose two or three eggs a week. We couldn't afford that.

For the next week, King was tied to the clothes post. Nothing more was said about it, and Gene and I assumed all was forgotten. The next week, a man who worked with Pa came over to our house. We were leaving to see the movies, and Pa gave Gene and me fifteen cents each. When we came back, King wasn't tied to the clothes post. We called but couldn't find him.

We hadn't been told that Pa was going to give him away. We both cried to get him back, but it was too late. It hurt us deeply.

Pa explained that King could have either been put to sleep or given to a good home. We couldn't afford to keep such a big dog. I always felt that Grandpa Phillips had pushed Pa into this decision because even Pa was sad about it for days. The next week, he came home with a little fox terrier puppy we called Pepper, but it was never the same without King.

The End of Our First Year

We had done it. We made it through the first year. I would soon be going to kindergarten, and I was looking forward to that. One Saturday, we had nothing pressing. We had over 300 chickens, but no produce to pick, so Pa woke us early for our weekend fishing. For several weeks, Pa would take us fishing in Hustisford or Mud Lake every Saturday and Sunday after church.

Our folks loved to pack a picnic lunch with soda and beer and find a park to spend the day at. Even when we would fish, Gene would go off by himself. I loved to fish, but it was more special to be together and have a good time. Pa was always good-natured, and Grandpa Phillips was, too. I hadn't been in trouble or lost for such a long time, and I think that made everyone happy.

I was still weak because of my sickness. I slept more, rested more, and tired more easily. I didn't realize it, but my family did. They always tried to encourage me to sit down and read. They even had me start piano lesson lessons, but I wasn't talented like Gene. Gene was always good with music, and when he started playing the trumpet, he was the best.

But right now, we didn't have to worry about produce or getting wood for the winter because we were having a picnic. With the money we earned that summer, Pa had the furnace fixed and bought two tons of coal for the winter. The only thing I had to dread about the winter was still walking out to the outhouse in the snow. ☆✧

Chapter Three | 1937–1938
The Family

Happy Nothings Day

Friday was the best day of every week. Pa got paid on Fridays, and after dinner we would all dress up and go to downtown West Allis for our weekly shopping. Sometimes Pa would surprise us with gifts after dinner. He called it "Happy Nothings Day." One time, both of us kids got a gold-plated toy motorcycle for a Harley Davidson anniversary. Mom and Evelyn both got nylon hose that were almost impossible to get. Grandpa Phillips got a small bottle of whiskey. He used to hide bottles all over the farm. Every time he took a swig, he would tell me not to tell Mom.

We did most of our grocery shopping at Genkee's Downtown Grocery, where we put the bill on a charge account. On Fridays, we went to A&P for items we couldn't get from Genkee's. Downtown was always busy on Friday nights. The biggest stores were JC Penney, Sears, and Woolworths, but we had a lot of local clothing stores as well. Sometimes we went to a movie but usually just stopped at Felton's A&W for a root beer and maybe a beef sandwich.

On Saturdays, Gene and I would go to the Capitol Theater or Allis Theater downtown. A movie was eight cents, and popcorn sold for a nickel. Sometimes Pa would give us each twenty-five cents for the movies. When that happened, we would stop at the New York Coffee Pot and get a hamburger for seven cents.

When Mom went back to work for a short time, we lived pretty well. She was talented and found work easily. Mom was a millinery designer and once had a chance to become a national designer for a big firm in New York. But she turned it down because she felt it would hurt her marriage and family. She took positions in upscale dress shops and taught for years at the YWCA in Milwaukee. She became a prominent person in Milwaukee and had appearances on WTMJ TV with Bob Heise, weekly radio, and fashion shows. She was a leader in the Red Feather Fund for Milwaukee, and she taught etiquette to debutants for their coming-out parties. She never discussed this with us, though. To us, she was just Mom who made the meals, cleaned the house, and worked in the fields.

Pa worked at Harley Davidson for many years as a set-up man and machinist. He only had a sixth-grade education but could build a house, repair the wires and plumbing, and tear down a car motor and put it together again. When Mom got her day jobs, Pa would cook the meals, clean the house, and do the washing and never complained.

Over the years, Pa opened a fish market, restaurant, and grocery store and made a profit in each. He could take a vacant building and design a layout and do all the buildouts himself. He had a great sense of humor and joked all the time. He had an incredibly positive attitude. If one of us kids was having a bad day or acting crabby, Pa would get all the kettles from the kitchen, and we would all use wooden spoons to pound on the kettles and parade around the house until we were laughing and happy again. Sometimes he would grab Mom, Gene, or me and lift us up and dance, carrying us around the room. He was a strong man; in fact, a professional wrestler had once said that my Pa was the strongest man he had ever met.

Mom and Pa never fought or said a bad word about each other. We were disciplined, but never in anger. Christ was the center of their lives and the center of our home.

Gene's First Job

It was still dark, but I heard Gene getting out of bed and dressing. It wasn't to do chores, but rather because it was his first day of work. It was the spring of 1940, and Bob was almost eleven years old. He was used to hard work and wanted to get a job bunching radishes or pulling weeds at a muck farm in Greenfield. He hated farm work but liked money to buy more pigeons. He and his buddy Donnie wanted to buy some new birds to show at the State Fair. The year before, they had both won a red ribbon. This year they were going for the ultimate blue ribbon.

Many of the older kids Gene's age worked at muck farms. They made good money, but it was hot work in the fields and long days. They were paid three cents for every bushel of radishes or carrots they pulled, and some kids made as much as twelve cents an hour.

Mom packed Gene a lunch and a note giving permission for him to work. That first day, I went with him to Greenfield Avenue to meet the truck. The corner was crowded with local kids all waiting to go to work. Some of the kids started shouting at me to go home to my mother. "You're just a runt," they yelled, "too small to be away from home."

Gene's friend Donnie was there waiting for him. Donnie was a skinny kid with glasses and not very strong. He was ill as a young kid and tired easily.

Shortly after, a great big truck came down Greenfield Avenue with a big wooden rack on the back for hauling cattle. The kids climbed up onto the truck after giving the farmer their notes from home. If you were too short or frail, you were sent home. All the kids had to stand up on the truck because it was too crowded to sit. What an exciting day! My brother had a real job!

When they got to the farm, each kid had to write his name on his lunch bag, and then everyone stacked the lunches in the shed. Each kid was given a number and assigned a row to work in. When you had filled your basket with produce, an older kid would take your number and run the basket back to the shed to get the radishes washed and bunched. Your number was put on a spindle and counted at the end of the day. If you averaged less than two bushels an hour, you couldn't come back.

Once the radishes were bunched, they were put into crates, and a man drove them to local stores to sell. Sometimes the driver would take one big kid along to deliver. Gene wanted that job because the driver would take that kid out for lunch.

On the very first day of work, Donnie got sick. He got dizzy from the heat and thought he was going to throw up. Gene told him to keep working or he would get fired. Donnie finished the day but turned in twelve bushels in nine hours. He was told not to come back.

Not surprisingly, Gene was one of the kids with the most bushels. Before kids went home, the farmer paid everyone. Gene went home with over $1.25 for just nine hours! He was really excited about being so rich.

The farm jobs lasted less than a week. Kids worked one farm field at a time, and once a field was finished, they waited until the next field opened up. Gene took his money and bought a prized pigeon for himself and one for his friend, Donnie. Donnie almost cried when they got the pigeons. They never did get a blue ribbon, but it was still a Blue Ribbon Day.

I Have a Bridge to Sell You

Both Mom and Pa trusted everybody. If any salesman came to our door, they could sell anything to my folks. Our door was practically open to every crook. Once, we bought a twelve-inch Zenith television that only lasted for one year. Mom saw an ad in

The Journal classifieds section for a guy who could fix televisions for cheap. He came to the house, looked at the TV, and said he would have to take it back to his shop to test it with his equipment. He never came back and neither did our TV!

Pa hired a neighbor to rewire the house. The neighbor worked on it every weekend for almost five months, and every weekend, my parents would pay him twenty dollars in cash for his work. After six months, he still wasn't finished. We finally called a licensed company to finish the job only to find out the company couldn't use any of our neighbor's work. Our neighbor had never wired a house before.

One day a man came to the door selling driveway repairs. We had a gravel driveway, and Pa wanted to have it covered with asphalt. He gave the man a $20 deposit. The man never came back.

The local furnace company said they could clean our furnace inexpensively. They tore off all the sheet metal and took down all the pipes in the basement. They then said they couldn't clean it because it was an unsafe furnace, but they could repair it for $100. We refused to have it fixed, and they refused to put it back together. My parents never got mad, though. They felt the company had lost more than money.

Did you want to sell a bridge?

Gene's Music

The Wendland family was always involved in music. Grandmother Wendland was an opera singer in Germany. After Grandfather Wendland moved the family to America, all the kids (my Pa and his siblings) picked up instruments and started a family band. They played at local dances and family special events.

After we went to a family reunion at Aunt Dottie's farm, Gene started to practice on our old piano that had moved with us from 56th. He learned to read music by himself and played well without lessons. Our cousins, Willie and Jim—Uncle Howard's kids—were older and could play the trumpet, clarinet, accordion, *and* the piano.

Pa contacted a well-known piano teacher in West Allis to give Gene lessons, but she wanted twenty-five cents an hour, and we couldn't afford that much. But after she heard Gene play, she offered to teach him for a dozen eggs. He hated our farm and the work, but he loved music.

Gene was selected to play in a city concert that focused on "future musician kids." He stole the show. After he played, everyone agreed he was the most talented.

Liberace was a famous pianist, born in West Allis, Wisconsin, to immigrants. Gene met him at our uncle Bob's club and followed him around like a shadow. Liberace was much older and naturally had a lot of responsibilities with his performances, but he encouraged Gene to follow his dream.

The Wendland cousins got together and decided to form a family band called the "Next Generation." It never came to fruition because of the Depression and families struggling just to survive. Gene's teacher stopped teaching him after two years because he had outgrown her capabilities. He was a better pianist than she was.

I started taking lessons, but there weren't enough eggs left for her to teach me. I did end up with a good voice, for which I'm thankful. So, when Gene played at church, I was selected to sing.

In 1947, Gene went to Nathan Hale High School and followed in the footsteps of cousins Willie and Jim. He took up trumpet and became the heartthrob of the school with his music. At sixteen, he formed his own band and played for weddings and special dances. By the time he graduated from high school, he sat in with the top bands in the country when they traveled to Milwaukee. *Downbeat*, a national magazine, publicized his talent, and he went on to travel with Red Nichols, a nationally renowned band leader.

When I entered Nathan Hale High, I took trumpet lessons to follow in Willie and Gene's footsteps. After a year in band, the prof recommended I quit and sign up for shop. He didn't realize I wasn't any good at shop either.

Gene found a love outside of his pigeons—music. He never told anyone he came from a small family farm and never wanted anyone of us to mention it. But he was happy, at last, and the folks were proud.

Gene and I Protest

During the Great Depression, we learned to eat anything that we could find. Most of our meals were made from the crops we had grown or our chickens and eggs. We lived much better than any of our city friends. But our selection of lunches and treats were still limited. When we came home from school and wanted a snack, we had bacon lard and radish or onion sandwiches. Once in a while, we had peanut butter that wasn't pasteurized, so it came with liquid on the top of the jar, and the rest was dry and stuck to the roof of your mouth.

The two things we hated the most were blood soup—made with duck blood—and liver. The blood soup was salty, and the liver was so dry it stuck in our throats. During the 1930s, we learned to shut our mouths and eat our meals. Table manners were particularly important. If you ate with your fingers, your hand would be hit with the backside of a knife. You never talked while adults were talking, and you always ate what was placed in front of you because people in other parts of the world—including our neighborhood—were starving.

One night, Mom made liver and onions, and Gene and I refused to eat it. Pa was easygoing, but not when it came to our refusal to eat a meal. We were told to leave the table and were not allowed to eat anything else that night. The next morning, we came back from our chores and had a cup of coffee. Grandpa Phillips and Pa were eating bacon, eggs, and freshly baked bread. It was common for parents to be served first. We were so hungry and ready for breakfast. Mom put our plates in front of us, and the liver from supper the night before stared back at us.

I finally ate the liver, all the while thinking I would choke to death. Have you ever had warmed up dry liver? Gene held out until lunchtime but also finally gave in. It was the one time I respected him. We never tried to refuse liver again, but we did get sneakier. We chewed the meat, and when the adults weren't looking, we gave it to the dog.

Pepper

We had a Fox Terrier named Pepper. He was Pa's dog and never left his side other than lunchtime when we fed him under the table. Pepper never left the farm other than a few weeks during the spring. He would take off for a week or two to "sow his oats," Grandpa Phillips said, whatever that meant! He always came back, though. He had been seen as far as two miles from the farm. Sometimes we would get calls from people telling us that if we didn't catch our dog, they would shoot him. Pa never went out looking for him because he knew Pepper would come home when he was ready. Sometimes he came home beaten up by other dogs, and once the dairy farmer two miles away called to say he had hit Pepper with a shovel when he chased his collie. He might have come home battered and bruised sometimes, but he would sleep for a week or two and regain his strength.

Pepper loved to go rabbit hunting, and sometimes, when Pa wasn't home, he would come out to the woods with us and chase rabbits. He must have caught at least a dozen rabbits, some fully grown and some babies, bringing them back and dropping them at our feet. The rabbits were in states of shock, but seldom bit or hurt.

One warm spring day, Pa was hoeing the raspberry bushes and mulching the plants with straw. Pepper was right there beside Pa, as always, waiting for a treat of summer sausage. Pa saw a grass snake crawling nearby and told Pepper to get the snake. They played this game all the time. Pepper would grab the snake by the back of the head, swing him around, and throw him up in the air. He would do this several times until the snake was dead. But this time, once the snake was dead Pepper started acting strangely. He wobbled back and forth and fell to the ground. Then he lay there, dead.

I started to cry, and Pa had tears in his eyes. He called to the dog, "Pepper! Pepper!" hoping he would respond. Several minutes went by, and we stood there looking at the dog.

Suddenly, Pepper opened his eyes and started to get up slowly as if drunk. Whatever had happened, that was the last time he chased snakes.

Country Life in the City

Even though we lived on a farm, we experienced some of city life, too. We lived three blocks from the bus stop and the State Fairgrounds, four blocks from the nearest grocery store, and could get weekly delivery services. We didn't have city water or sewer, though. It stopped one block from our farm.

When we first moved to the farm, we had a milkman come twice a week with his horse and carriage. Our iceman came twice a week to deliver fifty pounds of ice for our icebox. No one I knew had a refrigerator. The iceman had a horse and wagon and let kids sit on the back and get ice chips to suck on.

We always watched for the ragman each week. He was a fat, middle-aged man dressed in dirty overalls and a ragged shirt. He would always call out, "Dee rags! Dee rags!" He had an old horse and wagon filled with tin, rags, and lots of bundled-up newspapers. He came down to our basement and offered pennies for anything we had, mostly newspapers, rags, metal, or tin. He always paid less than the salvage yards and had a problem making correct change. He was always trying to short us.

One day, the ragman asked Pa if he had any pig iron. Pa didn't know what he meant by that. "Pig iron! Pig iron! That's all I want," said the ragman. He explained that the foundry made large steel casings and threw away the drop-offs with their sand waste. He told us they dumped off the sand and pig iron down the road from the farm. Some neighborhood kids dug through the sand and harvested the pig iron and sold it for cash. "Japan buys all they can get and pays a good price for it," the ragman continued. He didn't know why Japan wanted it, but it was worth money. Later in the day, Gene and I took our coaster wagons and two-bushel baskets down to the dump. The ragman was right—a lot of kids from Walker Street and 88th Street were digging in the sand and had bushels of iron.

We spent the whole afternoon digging in the sand and putting pig iron in our wagons. The next day, we took two full wagons of pig iron to the junkyard on National Avenue about a mile and a half from home. The owner came out, happy to see us, asked about Pa, and weighed our iron. We had over eighty pounds on the wagons and made nineteen cents. They paid over twenty-five cents per hundred pounds for any pig iron. For three hours of work, we made ten cents each.

When we went home and told Pa, he was shocked by how much we had made. The ragman paid only five cents per hundred pounds and took a long time to collect. The next day, we took our coaster wagons and wheelbarrow and filled them to the top. We took those home, and Pa filled baskets and small barrels with iron. A few days later, he drove it all down to the junkyard. We had over 400 pounds of iron and made over a dollar. We picked pig iron that whole summer. In early fall, Pa took it over to the junkyard with a trailer. Two years later, we found out why Japan wanted the iron.

The New Shower

It was Saturday morning in early July, and it promised to be a special day. For two years, Gene and I had taken turns taking baths in the wash tub in the kitchen with the family of spectators. Now was the day I would take my first shower.

Pa worked for a week installing the shower in the garage. He picked up a fifty-gallon barrel from the junkyard and drilled a hole in the bottom. Then he put the barrel on the garage roof and drilled a hole through the roof. He cut an old garden hose and stuck one end in the barrel and ran the other end through the roof into the center of the garage where we had a concrete floor. He attached a small showerhead to the end of the hose, and the shower was complete.

Then came the hard part. Gene and I had to fill pails of water from the house and carry them to the garage. Pa would carry each pail up the ladder and fill the barrel. This took two hours to do! We waited for hot weather to warm our water, and presto—we had a hot shower.

Now the day had finally come when we could use our new shower. Gene and I got into our swim trunks and ran out to the garage. Gene went first. Pa opened up the showerhead, and Gene soaped himself. Then Pa opened it up again, and Gene washed the soap off. I had to wait for my turn, but I was extremely excited. I couldn't wait to tell the kids at school that we had a shower.

When it was my turn, I felt like I had gone to heaven. The water was cold, but the weather was hot, so it felt really good. So far, this was the greatest thrill of my life. Finally, we had plumbing like everyone else. The next day, I told my friends in the neighborhood that we had our own shower, and they all laughed because they already had indoor plumbing.

For some reason we never used our shower again. Maybe it was because our well was going dry or because Gene didn't care to carry water for two hours to take a shower. I didn't care. It was still a special day.

New Neighbors

In the fall, Gene and I took care of the chickens and his pigeons and scraped off our shoes on the boot rail (a piece of sharp steel planted on the back door to clean off boots). One day, we saw people moving into the shack on the other end of the farm. The shack was vacant and partially falling down. Squatters had moved in and out of some of the other vacant houses in the area, but no one wanted to live in this shed. It was one of the hangout places for the local kids to smoke or do whatever they did. There was even one vacant house on McMyron Street where the owner had hanged himself in the basement. All the kids in the neighborhood broke into that house and showed their friends where the cut rope still hung from a rafter.

The shack next to our property was the worst in the neighborhood, though. Even our chicken coop was better than that. We went into our house to have breakfast and told Mom about the neighbors. She couldn't believe anyone could live in the shack. It didn't have a furnace or any plumbing and wasn't safe.

The next day, a new kid from the shack came over to introduce himself. His name was Georgie, and he had three sisters and three brothers, and his dad couldn't find work. They had lived in Hobo Junction on the tracks until they found this place. At least they would be inside in the winter. We were about to do our chores, so Georgie went to our chicken coop with us. When we opened the screen door to the coop and walked into what had been a kitchen, Georgie said that he hoped one day they could have a home as nice as that.

Most people were treated well by their neighbors, no matter how poor they were, but squatters were not treated well. Nobody trusted them, and everyone was afraid they would steal. People didn't lock their doors unless they knew there were squatters in the neighborhood.

Georgie was about ten years old, and his skin was dark with dirt. This was the first house his family had had in months, and they were so happy to have a roof—or part of one—over their heads. The whole family worked to clean out broken glass, water-soaked rugs, and broken furniture. An old well was positioned in the backyard, so the family cleaned out what they could and took water out to wash and clean. They didn't have heat, so they lit fires in old washtubs to heat the house. The only light they had was from candles.

Georgie spent most of his time at our house. I think it was to keep warm. At that time, many people spent their days in schools, churches, stores, or libraries so they could get warm.

Georgie's family was genuinely nice and never caused trouble. Everybody seemed to like them, and Mom and other ladies took them food and clothing for all their kids. Some of the neighborhood kids, however, made jokes about them and picked on them.

One day, the neighborhood kids decided to give Georgie a present for his birthday. His eyes lit up when they handed him the gift wrapped in pretty paper with a ribbon around it. He was so excited and carefully unwrapped the gift and ribbon so as not to damage his special gift. When he opened the gift, he looked into the box to see dog poop.

The other kids started laughing and thought it was so funny. Georgie never said a word. Tears crept out of his eyes, but he never said a word. Everybody stopped laughing, and no one spoke. It was the most shameful day of my life. The other kids had done this, but I was still present and a part of it. I was so ashamed of that day. I still am ashamed.

In the spring, the sheriff caught the family and moved them off the property, but it was the best winter they had had in years.

The Fourth of July

One month before my birthday, I had finally reached the day I might ride the rollercoaster. The midway on the state fairgrounds had rides and games that operated from Memorial Day until Labor Day on weekdays and weekends. I was only seven and not yet allowed to ride by myself. But my goal in life was to be tall enough to get onto the ride with someone else.

Every time we went to the midway at the fairgrounds, the workers asked me my age and then measured me. I had to be 4'10" tall to get on the ride. In another month, I would be eight, and I was almost tall enough.

Today was the Fourth of July. We packed a lunch to go see the parade and have a picnic at the fairgrounds. Gene was marching for the Boy Scouts in the parade with his best friend, Donnie. My cousins, Jim and Harry, were in the high school band, and Uncle

Howard was the postmaster for the VFW and was leading the veterans. It was a great day for the Wendlands!

After the parade, we went to the picnic grounds to have our lunch. In the few minutes after our lunch, the rides would open, and I would be able to ride the rollercoaster. Pa gave each of us fifty cents to go on ten rides. Gene and I ran over to the rollercoaster and bought tickets.

"How old are you, kid?" the man behind the stand asked.

"I'll be eight on August 28," I said.

"Okay, let's see how tall you are."

I stood as straight as I could, a little bit on my toes.

"Sorry, kid, you're too small. Come back next year."

Gene piped up and said he would take care of me, but the operator wouldn't give in. "It's for your own good, kid. Just be patient and wait until you're bigger."

I was so disappointed that I started to cry. We got a refund on our rollercoaster tickets and rode the Ferris wheel, Loop-de-Loop, and the Old Mill. But they weren't like the rollercoaster.

We stayed for fireworks. They were so close, we could almost touch them. But when we went home, I was very discouraged.

It was sometime later that summer that Gene, my cousin Denny, and I went to the fair. I hadn't grown much, so I never tried to get back on the rollercoaster again. We were walking to the picnic grounds when we saw someone flying off the rollercoaster as it came down the big drop. At first, we thought it was a package, but it was really a person. Gene wouldn't let us look.

That night, we told Mom, and she was glad the operator hadn't let me on the ride. The next day, The *Milwaukee Journal* told the story about a little eight-year-old boy who had slipped under the restraining bar and fell to his death. The operator was not at fault because the boy was eight years old and just 4'10" tall. I never wanted to ride the rollercoaster again and never did.

Here Today and Gone Tomorrow

I'll never forget the first Halloween on the farm. The year before, when I was only three years old, I had found the trick-or-treat candy and shared it with King. For whatever reason I didn't understand at the time, he got sick from it and pooped all over the living room rug. It made quite the mess, and everyone blamed me for what the dog had done. My name was never said only once. It was always repeated: "Eddie, Eddie, Eddie, what have you done?"

The year 1937 was different. I did nothing wrong, but Mom bought the trick-or-treat candy and then hid it. She didn't trust me. We got a great big pumpkin from my uncle Charles's farm. Gene and I carved a really scary face on the pumpkin and put it on the porch. He went out to trick or treat, and I stayed home to give out the candy. We only had a few kids come because we were the only farm on the block, and since we had just moved, people didn't know us yet. Grandpa Phillips sat and told me stories about when he was a kid and they used to take down their neighbor's outhouses on Halloween and put them on their front porches. I didn't know that grandpas were ever kids. I thought they were just always old. Grandpa Phillips checked the chicken coop before he went to bed, and then seeing everything was okay, he headed into the house. No one was around.

The morning after Halloween, Grandpa Phillips and I got up at dawn. He went out to check on the chickens, and I trotted out to the outhouse. As I walked around the machine shed, I stopped in my tracks. The outhouse was gone. All that remained was a big hole. It smelled really bad. How could the whole outhouse just up and leave? Maybe some of Grandpa Phillips's kid friends put it on the porch.

I ran to the front of the house, but the outhouse wasn't there. I ran into the house, shouting for Mom. Gene asked what was going on, and I told him someone had taken our outhouse. He called me a dork. I didn't even know what that meant. Mom heard us arguing over it, and I told her someone had taken our outhouse. "It's not even on the front porch," I said, breathless from the arguing. "And that's where they're supposed to put it. Grandpa Phillips told me!"

We went out to see what had happened. When Mom saw the big hole in the ground, she got really upset. Things like this had never happened in West Allis. We didn't even have a real police department to call. "How could anyone do this?" she exclaimed.

"Grandpa Phillips said they're supposed to put it on the porch, but they didn't," I reminded everybody.

When Grandpa Phillips got back from the chicken coop, we all went back outside, a little search party for the wooden shed where we did our business. It was still nowhere to be found. Pa got home from work that night, and he was mad. We searched the fields and woods. Nothing.

The next morning, someone from the neighborhood called and asked us if we'd lost an outhouse. Pa and Grandpa Phillips hooked the trailer onto the car and drove it over to the neighbors. The lady took us into her backyard, but the shed she had was an old one; it wasn't our outhouse.

Pa and Grandpa Phillips planned to build a new outhouse the following day. After breakfast, they picked up their tools in the machine shed and headed out to start on the project. As we walked around the shed, Grandpa Phillips said, "Welp, looks like we can put our tools back. Our outhouse came back home."

To this day, we've never been able to find out who took it or how it got back, but every year after, we guarded that little shed on Halloween.

Spring Cleaning

Spring had come to Wisconsin. It was the most wonderful time of the year. The birds were singing, and buds were beginning to shoot out of the dry, scraggly trees. Our land was plowed by a local farmer who owned a horse and plow. We had just bought 100 chicks for the year, and the world was good.

One Saturday morning, Mom woke us to get out of bed so she could wash the bedding and hang them outside. Evelyn started to take down the curtains and wash the windows. This was how spring cleaning always started. Because of this, Gene and I always wanted to get out of the house as fast and as far as we could. Just as we were heading out the door to escape, Mom caught us and called us back. She marched us into the kitchen, and no matter how much we fought, the inevitable was going to happen.

The "old-timers" believed that the body was polluted with poisons during the winter and had to be cleaned out in the spring to get the poison out. Their method of doing this was a large dose of castor oil. I noticed that my parents and grandparents didn't have to clean out their bodies; they never took castor oil. I believe it was a method of torture they inflicted upon us.

Castor oil was a fix-all. When a child had a stomachache, headache, or ingrown toenail, it was a result of needing a good, old-fashioned "clean-out." Even Grandpa Phillips turned on us and insisted we take our medicine. Each of us got two tablespoons of castor oil, and five or six hours after, all hell broke out. It was a day we never wanted to be far from the outhouse. If we didn't have a good enough clean-out to satisfy the grownups, they gave us castor oil again the next day. So, if we didn't have a good clean-out, we lied. To this day, I still hate the thought of spring. ☆☆

Chapter Four | 1938
School Days

Back to School

Summer was over. The work was done on the farm, and we looked forward to school because the rooms were warm in the winter. A week before school started, Mom took us to downtown West Allis to get new jeans and our one new pair of shoes for the year. We also bought all our school supplies: pencils and writing tablets with nice cardboard back covers. The back cover was very important because when our shoes wore out, we cut the cardboard out to be used for an inner sole to stop water from coming into the shoe. Good cardboard could also be traded for marbles, penny gum, or baseball cards you could flip.

We played "kills" or flipped baseball cards on the way to school. Baseball cards were always attached to the three strips of gum we could buy for a penny. The gum companies couldn't get the gum to sell for a penny, so they thought they would throw in a baseball card for a professional team. We liked the gum, but the cards were worthless to us. None of us had ever heard of Babe Ruth or Lou Gehrig, so we flipped the cards. If you got heads, you won; if you got tails, you lost. Nobody ever kept the dumb cards. Sometimes we played marbles, too. A kid would throw down a marble, and the second kid had to hit it by shooting it off his fingers. That was called "kills."

All the neighborhood kids had to walk through our driveway and down the path through the woods to get to school. Gene and

I joined them as they passed through our farm. When the school bell rang, all the boys lined up to remove their slingshots, and the teacher put them away until we went home. We all carried pocketknives but had to keep them in our desks. Mom didn't like knives, so she would take my knives and hide them because she didn't want us to get hurt. Grandpa Phillips always just bought me new knives and gave them to me on the sly. "Don't tell your mom," he'd say.

When the bell rang at the end of the day, the teacher returned our slingshots, and we shot squirrels and birds on our way home. The knife was a necessity. We used it to play Mumbly Peg, or to cut branches for fishing poles, or to make bows and arrows. A boy couldn't live without his own knife.

Many times, we would have "social disagreements" on the way home. Today, one would call these disagreements "fights," but back then, we viewed them no differently from playing football, baseball, or pom-pom pull-away. You could get hurt in any sport, and social disagreements were a sport.

Our school was only a short distance from our house. We walked through our woods and down a half-mile dirt alley right to the school door. It only took fifteen minutes to get to school, but we always stayed for lunch. The lunch program was two cents a day, plus one cent extra for milk. We had some form of rice and cheese for every meal because it all came from the government. We had rice soup, rice pudding, rice burgers, or Spanish rice in addition to brick, cheddar, or Swiss cheese on white bread. It was a hot meal, and it was cheap. When we went home after school, we ate radish, onion, and lard sandwiches or dried-out peanut butter sandwiches if we were hungry. We liked the lard with salt the best.

Our school was a small two-story building with eight small classrooms and an attached wooden building for the third and fourth grades. The playground was made of gravel and stone, but we normally played in the large vacant lot next to the school called the "free-for-all field." Most of the boys in fourth grade and up used the field for wrestling. Every able-bodied boy spent his recess in the field wrestling. If you took one step into the wrestling field, you got hit or pushed over, and then the fight began. You were fair game for anybody.

Of course, we had rules for these fights! No kicking, biting, or spitting ever, and no hitting when your opponent was down. As soon as you said "uncle," the other kid had to stop fighting. We got a few busted noses, cut lips, and, occasionally, a broken arm or wrist. But nobody got really hurt. These were just social fights. We had a lot of those. They were great fun. To us, it was like playing on the monkey bars or the swing set. This was our playground. When recess was over, the vice principal would come down to the field to watch us wrestle around and then inform us that recess was over.

Sometimes we got into some pretty good social disagreements. The kids who went to the little private school down the road liked to come over to our school to taunt us because they got out twenty minutes earlier than we did. My class was in the barracks—the wooden building. The kids from Little Flower school would throw stones or mud at the windows of the wooden building. Mrs. Marvin (whom I really liked) would tell us we could get out early and "give those boys a lesson." Man, we would run out that door and jump those kids until they didn't know what hit them.

I was in a tough class. Several of my classmates had gone to the private school and had been thrown out for fighting or causing trouble, so they were one or two years older than the rest of us. We tended to fight for about a half an hour or until we all got tired and had to go home to dinner. At the end of the fights, we would all say goodbye and "we'll see you next week." No one was really hurt. The private school kids would even tell us we should thank them for helping us get out of school early.

Our school was not one of the better schools, education-wise. I was in the top of my class, and Gene was in the top of his, but probably because most of the other kids came from bad homes. Many of the families in the area were well within the poverty class, and the fathers (as I was told) were either drunks or didn't want to work, and the children had no supervision. Many of the boys had gone to the private school and either failed or were thrown out because of getting in trouble. The girls often didn't take baths, and because of this, they smelled and weren't always clean. Several girls were picked on at school for "selling favors." I didn't know what favors were, but I knew they must have been bad.

Jerry's Crow

One kid in my class, Jerry, had a pet crow. It was a pretty bird and would follow Jerry around wherever he went. Sometimes Jerry played at my house, and he always brought his crow. The crow was not allowed to come to school because once he had disrupted the class. So, the crow stayed home.

Several times, however, the crow managed to get out and showed up at school. He would caw outside our window, "Oh, Jerry! Oh, Jerry!" over and over until Mrs. Marvin told Jerry to take his crow home. Jerry walked outside, and the crow would sit on his shoulder, and they would go home together.

My Best Friend

Richie Stark was my neighbor and best friend. I was told that he had had polio when he was a baby, so one of his legs was shorter than the other, and he couldn't walk well. One day, my third-grade teacher told Richie to leave the room and sit in the hall. Since the third- and fourth-grade classrooms were in the barracks, they had very little heat. The hallway in between the classrooms had no heat and was always freezing.

My teacher told the class that Richie was possessed by the devil, and he was evil and that was why he was crippled. She told us that none of us should play with him. I was a shy kid and very seldom spoke in class. (In fact, I was sent to a special reading class because everybody thought I couldn't read. The reading teacher sent me back to class with a note saying I didn't read out loud because I was scared, but I was actually an excellent reader.) Even though I was shy, I jumped out of my seat that day and screamed at the teacher, "Richie had polio and isn't evil! You're a liar! He's not evil." The teacher grabbed me by the back of the collar and dragged me out of the room, said I was possessed by the devil, and was evil as well.

Richie and I sat in the coatroom hallway for the rest of the afternoon. It was snowing outside and freezing in the hallway. We got so chilled that we huddled in the corner and covered ourselves with a stack of coats to keep warm. I didn't tell Gene on the way home, but I was so chilled to the bone, I couldn't warm up. I didn't tell Mom because I was ashamed of myself for shouting at the teacher, even though I hated her. My teacher was always mean and often hit kids with a big ruler or dragged them out of class by the backs of their collars. I was very quiet, and Mom asked what was wrong. "Nothing," I answered.

About two hours after we got home from school, Mrs. Stark called and told Mom what had happened to Richie. She said, "You must be very proud of Eddie for standing up to the teacher for Richie." Mom was really upset when I told her the whole story. She went to the principal the next day.

This was the first time Mom was mad enough to go to the principal. As it turned out, several teachers in our school, including my teacher, never had licenses to teach. They didn't even have college educations and had only gotten their jobs at farm schools because of personal friends.

I'll never know what happened between Mom and my teacher. But when school let out in the spring, my teacher was gone. From that day on, Mom ran the PTA and was influential in the school. She was a smart lady and well-known for her TV and radio experience as well as her years of working as head of the YWCA training program. Needless to say, Gene and I never had trouble again.

A Non-Social Disagreement

It took me several years to get over my health problems that had arisen from rheumatic fever, and I still tired easily. By the time I was eight years old, though, I felt pretty well. I ran and played as much as everybody else. Now the fun began.

Doug Wyatt was a year older than I and went to the same church as my family. For some reason—probably just his attitude—he got mad at me one day and chased me home from school. He caught me just across the field from home and started to knock me down and beat the tar out of me. I could tell from my bloody nose that this was not a usual social disagreement. This guy wanted to seriously hurt me.

I didn't think it was nice to beat up a member of the same church. Plus, at that time I wasn't really a fighter. I was pretty cowardly. After getting slapped around for about ten minutes, I had had enough. I did what any able-bodied fighter would do; I told him to let up because I had to be home for supper. This made sense to Doug, and after a few more whacks, he let up.

When I got home, I had a black eye, a bloody nose, and a body covered in mud. Mom was really upset. Her sick little baby had gotten hurt. She cleaned me up and gave me an ice pack to put on my bloody nose. "Don't ever fight, Eddie," she told me. I didn't cry at home, but I had cried like a baby when Doug pounded me.

Pa didn't say a word in front of Mom, but he walked outside with me and told me the facts of life. "Never let someone pound on you, or everyone will do it. What do you think Doug is telling the other kids? You're going to be a punching bag for the neighborhood. I never want you to start a fight, but I never want you to run away from one. I hope this never happens again."

I only had one real fight after that, and I lost to three bigger guys. But I had plenty of social disagreements, and I never backed down on those.

The Boxing Lesson

It was recess time on an early fall day. All the kids ran down to the free-for-all field to have a social fight. I loved the sport because it let me practice my form of judo. I was fighting with several kids when Dick Middlen grabbed me by the front of my shirt and socked me in the jaw. I never liked fighting with Dick or his brother because they were tough and dirty fighters. If they lost, they would gang up on you. Dick was two years older than me but in the same class.

I grabbed his arm and threw him over my back. Dick thumped to the ground like a bag of cement, flat on his back. I knew that I was in trouble. He got to his feet, swearing and swinging his fists like a madman. I just tried to hold him off when Mr. Janis came over to tell us recess was over.

Thank God, the fight was over. I didn't want to fight with him. I headed for the playground, which was out-of-bounds for fights, when Dick jumped my back and started beating me on the back of the head. I knew Dick wasn't going to forget what I had done.

Mr. Janis grabbed each of us by the arms and walked us back to school, down the stairs, and into the gym. All the kids followed us. He picked up two pairs of boxing gloves and said, "Okay, boys, we'll give you a chance to fight it out." I didn't really want to fight. Dick was older than me, and he was nuts! Plus, he was tough. Many of the kids stayed away from Dick and his brother because they never knew what they would do.

Mr. Janis put a pair of boxing gloves on me, and that was when I realized I was as good as dead. I made believe that I was ready to fight. Pa had said I should never back down, but I came close this time. Then Mr. Janis grabbed the second pair of gloves to put on Dick.

Dick started backing up and kept saying, "I don't want to fight Eddie."

Mr. Janis grabbed Dick's arm and finished tying the gloves on. Dick's face twisted and he pulled away, crying, "I don't have to fight, and you can't make me!"

Mr. Janis said, "I thought you wanted to kill Eddie. Now you don't. Are you sure?"

Dick didn't answer. He just kept crying.

All of the kids who had followed us to the gym were shocked. Pa was right. Because I didn't back down, I gained the respect of the school, and the Middlens never bothered me again. Thank God, because Dick would have killed me.

The Honor System

Those of us living during the Great Depression had very little money, but those who lived on a farm always had enough food. By our second year of living on our farm, we had added several hundred chickens and increased our work land to over ten acres. It didn't matter that all our neighbors were scraping the bottom financially; we trusted them. We never locked our doors. In fact, we didn't even have a key for our door. If we weren't home, visiting neighbors would just walk in to drop something off, or else they would put a pot of coffee on the stove while they waited for us to return.

When our apples were ripe, neighborhood kids would climb the fence or break it down to pick a few apples. When Pa caught them, he told them to come through the yard to get the apples, but not to break the fence. He always felt we could share a few apples with our neighbors.

One day, Grandpa Phillips and I went out to feed the chickens and found the door partly opened, and the snow drifted into the feed room. He asked me if I had been in the coop, but I hadn't. Then we found an envelope on the feed barrel and inside was a note. It said that a chicken had been taken for food but was only signed "from a friend." The mysterious thief must not have closed the door when they left. We went back to the house, and Grandpa Phillips showed the note to Pa.

Grandpa Phillips never said a word to us about the situation, because adults never explained anything to children. Ten days later, another envelope was placed on the feed barrel, and inside we found nickels, dimes, and pennies.

Every two weeks after that, we found envelopes with change, but no letter. This happened about six or seven times, and then they stopped coming. If Pa or Grandpa Phillips ever found out who the anonymous "friend" was, they never told us. Pa always said, "Many of us today don't have money, but we have honor, and our neighbors have honor."

Patty's Ponytail

When I moved up into the first grade, I thought I was big stuff—truly a grownup! I had my very own desk with an inkwell and could open my desk by myself to store my books and papers.

My desk was in the last row next to the window, and a little girl named Patty sat in front of me.

I didn't like girls back then. They were dumb, ran funny, and couldn't throw a baseball. But for some reason, I liked Patty. Maybe it was because of her long, brown hair that flowed down to her waist, or maybe because she smelled so good (I concluded that she must have taken a bath more than once a week). But I never told my friends my thoughts because they would laugh at me. The problem after that year was that I never seemed to get over that attraction for girls!

Patty had a long ponytail that draped over the top of my desk. When she turned her head from side to side, the tail would brush over my desk like a flyswatter. I was always a shy boy and seldom got yelled at by my teachers, but that ponytail just tempted me to give it a tug.

Patty would swing around and shout, "Eddie, don't do that! Don't pull my hair!" For some reason, I liked hearing her scold me. That was the only time she talked to me. She was the popular girl, you see, and I was the shrimp of the class.

No girls ever talked to me, and if they had, I wouldn't have known what to say. But sometimes I think Patty purposefully moved her head side to side to tease me. Not that a girl would *ever* tease a boy.

Or would they? I would find out later in life.

Then something happened. We came back to school right after Christmas break, and we all had to write a story about what we had done for Christmas. But we weren't allowed to mention the gifts we had gotten because some of the kids in the class didn't get gifts and would have felt bad. I was lucky because I always got a gift from my folks and a gift from Santa.

The teacher was going to take all our stories and make a Christmas book for the class. She would select two children to run the papers off on the mimeograph machine. It was in the old closet with an overhead lightbulb and no windows. The students would have to pour ammonia into a tray and then turn the handle several times to run off one copy. It was like magic. The closet had no vents, so sometimes a kid would get dizzy and need to sit in the hallway for a few minutes. It would take several hours to run off the twenty-four Christmas books, and everyone wanted that job to get out of class.

I had just filled my fountain pen, and ink started dripping on my paper. Sometimes, our filled pens would drip onto our desks, and we would have to wash them off with a soapy rag. After I cleaned my desk, I forgot to cover the inkwell. Patty turned her head from side to side, and her ponytail just dropped right into my inkwell. When her hair moved side to side again, ink started running down her back.

I poked Patty to tell her, and when she stood up, the ink on her hair ran down the back of her skirt. She started shouting, "Eddie, you did this!"

She kept crying, and the teacher ran over with a towel to wipe off her hair and back. Patty's mother was called, and she went right home.

I just forgot to cover my inkwell. It was an accident, but Patty never forgave me. Later that year, she gave all the kids valentines except for me. She was moved to a new desk away from me, and she came back to school one day with a short haircut. Now I couldn't pull her hair or hear her holler at me anymore.

But she still smelled nice.

A New Kid

It was the fall of my second-grade year. Mrs. Carter walked into the classroom with a little girl who wore a blue dress so long it almost covered her brown boy's shoes and her toes sticking out. The dress was dotted with large white flowers and so big it must have belonged to her mother. The little girl had messy brown hair that covered her face and hung over her shoulder.

"This is Shari Bunn, class," Mrs. Carter said. Shari looked down as if embarrassed by her boy's shoes. She made her way to her newly assigned seat across from me, and the girls in the classroom started snickering. I didn't say anything in my shyness. An awful smell began to fill the room. We soon realized it was the new little girl.

When we went outside for recess, Shari stayed by herself next to the school entrance. The other girls kept looking at her and laughing under their breath. I felt sorry for her because I knew how hard it was for new kids to come to a new place, but I didn't know what to say.

Things didn't get better as school progressed through the year. Shari smelled so bad that the kids would rub their hands on each other and say they were spreading "Shari B's germs." I am ashamed to say that I did it, too. I should have known better. As if she couldn't hear what we were saying or wasn't capable of lifting her head, Shari just looked down while we laughed at her expense. I don't think anyone said a nice word to her that whole year.

During wintertime, she wore a small, torn, dirty jacket over her blue dress. One day, Mrs. Carter told Shari to stay after class. I was cleaning the chalkboard and was the only other person in the room. The teacher opened up a large shopping bag and pulled out a dark red wool coat that she asked Shari to try on. Shari started to cry as she tried on the new coat. When she thanked Mrs. Carter, it was the first time I heard her speak. I looked at Shari in a new light. She had big, pretty brown eyes that stood out on her pretty face. She was a very beautiful girl.

After she left, Mrs. Carter asked me to be kind to Shari because she was having a hard time. I looked down because I knew Mrs. Carter knew I was also guilty. I was very ashamed. I don't know why we picked on Shari. None of us had new clothes. We all wore our brother's or sister's hand-me-downs. None of us had soles left on our shoes. Some of the other school kids lived in garages or came from squatter families. We had nothing to brag about. Her life may have even been worse. Perhaps she didn't have a mother or father or was a foster child. We knew how badly they were treated. But in second grade, we didn't think those kinds of things through.

When we all moved into the third grade, we had a cruel teacher who joined us in poking on the little girl with the blue dress and holes in her shoes. One day, Shari didn't show up for school. We didn't know what had happened, but we no longer had anyone to snicker at and no one's feelings to hurt. We soon forgot Shari and looked for another victim. It isn't a nice memory.

Are We Poor?

Every Thursday, the whole family went to the movies. On that day each week, theaters gave out dishes, glasses, or another part of a dinnerware set. If you went once a week, you could collect a complete set, given enough time. We always went to a theater near a hill because that made it easier to push the car to get it started.

The closest theaters to our home were the Allis and Capitol theaters, but we had to push the car almost two blocks to get it started if we went to one of those.

This particular week, we were going to the Paradise Theatre because it was located on a big hill, and Mom was collecting a set of dishes from them. The two weeks before, we hadn't gone to the movies, so Mom wouldn't collect a full set of dishes. When we asked why we had missed, Mom said she had had too much work to do.

That Saturday, when Gene and I went to the movies, Pa only gave us a dime each. That was just enough to get into the movies, but we wouldn't be able to buy popcorn or snacks or anything. When Gene asked if we could have a nickel more, Pa got mad at us. Pa never got mad at anything.

Pa held out his hands and said, "Here's nothing. Take all you can." Pa had never gotten like that before. Something was wrong.

Gene and I went to his room to decide what to do. Neither one of us had a penny to our names, and it was too late to raise a nickel. We decided to go to the movies without buying popcorn. The Allis had a matinee special, which would cost us only eight cents total, leaving us with four cents to spend between us. It wasn't enough to buy popcorn, and hamburgers were seven cents each. What should we do?

Then, before we had gone through the queue and bought our tickets, Gene told me to go into the alley in the back of the theater and wait for him. I didn't know why, but he had some plan. I stood at the exit door for several minutes and waited for Gene. Where was he?

Suddenly, the exit door opened, and Gene whispered, "Get in here, quick!"

I ran through the door, and Gene pushed me into a seat. He looked around to see if an usher had seen us. We were safe.

"Gene," I squirmed, "I didn't pay to get in."

"Shut up, Eddie!"

I had never snuck into the movies before, and I was certain we would be arrested and go to jail.

We saw three movies, two fifteen-minute series, and five cartoons. We both bought popcorn and penny candy. It was wrong, and we never did it again. But it turned out to be a good day. We never told Mom or Pa because they would have made us go back to the theater and pay the eight-cent admission price for each of our tickets.

The following Monday morning, Mom didn't give us money for hot lunch while we got ready to go to school. Each one of us would usually receive fifteen cents a week for lunch and a pint of milk. Instead, Mom packed a bag lunch for each of us. When we asked, she said we were probably tired of rice for every meal, and the bagged lunch would give us a nice change. We complained that the "nice change" meant we'd have to eat a lard sandwich or that dried-out government peanut butter that stuck to the roofs of our mouths. She snapped back at us to "be glad you have something to eat."

Something was wrong. She never snapped at us.

When I got to school, I told my friends how Gene and I had snuck into the movies. Nobody was impressed because they had all snuck in before.

When the teacher came around to collect lunch money, I didn't have any. My teacher asked if my mother had just forgotten, but I told her we were tired of rice and wanted a homemade sandwich.

"Most people are poor today and can't afford hot lunches," my teacher said.

"But, we're not poor, Mrs. Baker," I said. "We'd rather have sandwiches."

"Okay, Eddie. It's okay."

My face got red and hot. We weren't poor.

When we got out of school, I ran to catch up with Gene and his friends. Gene never wanted to walk with me because he said I was a nuisance. I told Gene what Mrs. Baker had said, like she thought we were poor.

"You dope!" Gene laughed. "What? Did you think we were rich? You got hand-me-down shoes with holes in them! We live in a rundown dump, and we eat lard sandwiches."

I just stood there as Gene kept walking with his friends. I had never thought we were poor. To be poor was a bad thing. Nobody had ever told me we were poor before.

I ran the rest of the way home to ask Mom. She would know.

"Eddie, you're out of breath." Mom met me at the house. "You shouldn't run so much. The doctor told you not until you're fully well."

"Mom, are we poor?" I gasped. "The teacher said we were poor, and I asked Gene, and he said we were poor."

As if I had said a dirty word, Mom swung around. "Gene told you that? He should know better. No, Eddie, we're not poor. We have a home, food, clothing, our health, and each other. No, we're not poor and never will be because we also have faith. 'Poor' is when you have lost your faith, and we will never do that. If you plan to be a minister, don't ever forget what I've said."

We went financially broke several times after that, but Mom was right: we were never poor.

Napoleon

My books and pencils were put away in my desk, and I was waiting for school to be let out. The bell rang at 3:10 p.m., but sometimes the teacher let us out early. It was a mild day in late November, just two days before Thanksgiving. I couldn't wait to get out of school because Napoleon would be waiting for me.

Last spring, Pa and I were at Reimer's Feed Mill to pick up chicken feed. We no longer had the large flock of chickens we once had; we cut the numbers down to only twenty-five layers for ourselves. We bought a hundred pounds of feed and threw it in the back of the car. Reimer's had boxes of baby chicks and ducks for sale and about a dozen goslings left. Pa bought a pair of geese, and I carried them home on my lap covered with a rag.

When we got home, we took some fencing and put it around the doghouse, a perfect place for the two geese. After two days, the goose got sick and died, but I still had the gander. The gander was lonely, so I spent most of my summer days sitting and playing with him. I named him Napoleon because he was small but brave.

Every day, Napoleon called for me when he was in the doghouse: "Come out and play!" When he was out of the fence, he would follow me wherever I went and sit right next to me. He used to show love for me by rubbing his neck up and down my leg and nibbling at my arm—never biting, just pinching as his way of kissing. When I was at school, I put him in the garage, and when he heard me coming down the path from the woods, he started honking for me. He was my best friend.

Sometimes, I would bring home a friend from school and tell Napoleon to get my friend. He chased my friend around the garage, and then I would stop him and let my friend pet him. It was mean of me, but my friends never got hurt, and they always liked petting the gander.

Back to the fall day. I ran down the alley to the woods after school. I don't know why I was so excited to see Napoleon again—I saw him every day. I ran down the winding path in the woods that everyone used to get home. The trees had retired for the year, and the branches were ready for winter. I knew once I reached the driveway my pet would start honking, but today, he was quiet. I opened the garage door, expecting him to fly all over me and give me kisses, but he wasn't there.

Maybe he was playing hide-and-seek in the bales of straw. I looked all over, but he wasn't to be found. I started to panic and thought he might have gotten out and gone to the woods looking for me. Sometimes, he would do that, but I worried that a dog had gotten him, or a hunter might have shot him, thinking he was wild. I called and called, but he never answered.

Tears formed in my eyes and ran down my cheeks. I ran to the house, crying, "Mom, I can't find Napoleon. I looked all over, and I can't find him."

Mom was surprised at my crying. "Eddie, we butchered him for Thanksgiving," she said with no emotion in her voice. "That's why we bought him after all. We thought you understood."

"You killed my best friend!" I shouted. "How could you do that?"

I could not believe it. I ran outside to the garage and hid in the corner until nightfall. I heard Mom and Grandpa Phillips calling me, but I never answered. I had just lost my best friend.

Years later, when I had a farm in Watertown, and Pa worked with me, a gander adopted him and followed him around and loved him as Napoleon loved me. Pa called him Alexander. One day, a new dog we had gotten attacked Alexander, and he eventually died. I felt sorry for Pa because I knew how he felt. I, too, had lost my best friend. ✩✩

Chapter Five | 1939
Christmastime

Christmas Parade

It was Saturday morning, and I woke up to the smell of eggs cooking and coffee brewing on the wood stove. Pa always did the cooking on Saturdays so Mom could get a day off. In the morning, he made his famous French toast or eggs-in-a-basket. For supper, his special was vegetable soup and butter burgers. I jumped out of bed and put on my Sunday dress clothes because this was a very special day.

Every year on the Saturday after Thanksgiving, we went to downtown Milwaukee to see the Schuster's Christmas parade with Santa Claus and Billie the Brownie, a little elf created by Schuster's Department Store. On Billie's head perched a green and red pointed hat with a ball of white fluff at the tip. Every Monday, I heard Santa and Billie the Brownie on the radio. A man named Larry did a show on WTMJ in Milwaukee, and he read letters from kids who contacted Santa and Billie at the North Pole. I never missed a radio show. In fact, I sent my own letter to Santa, but it was never read on the air.

Mom, Gene, and I took the 84th Street bus to Wauwatosa to catch the Rapid Transit Train. It took only fifteen minutes from 84th Street to get downtown. When we got off the train, Gene and I ran three blocks to Gimbels Department Store. It was only 9 a.m., but a large crowd had already formed for the unveiling of the Christmas windows and the magical world that would appear.

In one window, little elves made toys and gifts and loaded Santa's sled. Santa was sitting on the sled, and we could hear him laughing as if he were real. All the figures moved their arms and legs. We could hardly believe they weren't alive. On the other side of the entrance, figurines of little children skated on a pond and made a snowman. To us, it was like magic.

The doors opened at 9:30 a.m. Gene and I rushed across the main floor to walk on the moving stairs. The stairs came out of the floor and went up to the second level, then right back into the floor and disappeared. This was a strange and mysterious phenomenon! We ran up the down stairs and took them back to the first floor, and then they were gone. A mean-looking man in a uniform told us to get off the escalators, whatever those were.

Mom returned from the hosiery department. She had been looking for nylons, something new, and women would stand in line for hours to buy a pair. She told us it was time to see Toyland. The whole third floor had been transformed into Christmas City. Dozens of decorated trees held ornaments from all over the world. Gold garlands and huge ornaments and bells hung from one end of the building to the other. Electric trains ran on the floor, and one was suspended from the ceiling. Bikes and trikes lined up on one side of the room with dolls and stuffed animals on the other side. It would take a whole day to see everything in the room. I had never seen so many toys in my life, nor did I believe I would ever get one to keep. I think the store put them out mostly for show, because who would ever be able to afford them?

When it was time to leave, we took the elevator down to the first floor. A man dressed in a uniform and a red cap ran the controls. He asked if we would like to go up to the eighth floor and back down again, and he didn't charge us any money to do so. We went up very quickly, and it was lots of fun.

The parade started at 2 p.m., so we had time to go to Woolworths for a grilled cheese and an ice cream soda (with two scoops of ice cream!). We hurried out to the street and found a good spot on the corner. It was cold outside, and it had started to snow.

The parade started with two police cars leading the way. Then bands and floats and lots of music followed. Soon the crowd started to scream. A large float was coming our way, and on it sat Santa, Billie, and the reindeer. I was so close to the float that Santa looked right at me as I shouted and waved to him. It all went too fast.

Gene kept telling me the man in the parade wasn't Santa because there was no real Santa; he was only make-believe. Mom told Gene not to say that. "Leave Eddie alone," she said. When the parade was over, everyone rushed to get home. The depot was crowded, and we had to wait for a later train because the first one was full. On the next train, we stood all the way to 84th Street. Once we reached home, Pa had the soup on the stove and started the butter burgers.

I told Grandpa Phillips about the exciting day and how the department store stairs came out of the floor. He asked me if I saw Toyland and which toy I wanted Santa to bring me. No one ever had asked us kids that before. We had looked at those toys, but never expected to get one. I didn't know. "Whatever Santa brings me," I answered. Gene just laughed at me and told me I was a stupid baby. Then I got scared because Gene always knew more than I did.

"Grandpa," I asked, "is there a real Santa?"

"If you believe Santa is real, there is a Santa," he answered. I knew Grandpa Phillips wouldn't lie, so Santa was real. I felt sorry for Gene when Santa would find out what he had said.

Saint Nick's Day

December 5 came a week after the Christmas parade, and we celebrated it as the eve of Saint Nicholas Day. Saint Nick was a Dutch saint who brought candy and cookies to good children.

We put socks out, and Saint Nick always filled them. Since our socks were very small, Mom said we could use a pair of her old hose. Gene didn't want to leave socks out because he didn't believe in Saint Nick or Santa. He didn't even believe in the tooth fairy, and I had just gotten a nickel for my old tooth!

I woke up in the middle of the night and just lay in bed thinking about Saint Nick. At dawn, I ran into the dining room and found my hose on the piano bench. It was full, with a big apple, orange, hard candy, and nuts. I was rich!

Gene had finally left his hose on the buffet but came in only to find it under the piano stool. When he picked it up, it was full of charcoal. He was so mad he threw the hose across the room in a rage. He grumbled his way to school that day, grumpy and curt with everyone who may have been involved in his getting only charcoal.

When we got home after school, Gene went to lay his school clothes on his dresser, all folded up in a pile like we'd been taught to do. There he found his stocking full of candy. He mumbled a soft "thank you" to Mom and Pa, but he never again told anyone in the family he didn't believe in Saint Nick! Lesson learned.

Christmas Gifts

There were only two weeks left until Christmas, and it was time to prepare our gift lists. The older people worked on their gifts for weeks, but we kids always started ours after Thanksgiving. I had Mom, Pa, Grandpa Phillips, Gene, and Evelyn to make gifts for. We always made a present for our moms at school, so that left me with four more. I got Gene a new comic book that he didn't have. I traded two comic books and twelve marble shooters with Carolanne from school for one *Superman* comic book. It was costly, but I knew Gene would like it. Trading comic books was a game I could master. I had a dozen kids with whom I traded weekly, and I usually came out better on the deal.

For Evelyn, I took an old cigar box and covered it with colored paper for her jewelry. Mom helped me mix some white flour with water to make glue to paste on the paper. A large jar of paste cost five cents or more, so we made our own. Grandpa Phillips was very special, and I took a little more time on his present. Gene cut off a long willow branch, and I cut off the leaves until I had a long pole. Every time I got a piece of string, I saved it for future use. Everybody saved everything in case they could make something out of it in the future. When I had one long, fine string, I tied it to the end of the pole. Pa gave me a large fishhook and tied it to the end of the string. I found a cork near the railroad tracks and cut a hole through its center. I placed a part of the string into the hole and put in a stick to hold it. If he wanted, Grandpa Phillips could take the stick out and set the cork bobber at any height. I found a tiny piece of pig iron and added that for a sinker. It was perfect. Grandpa Phillips would love his fishing pole. Finally, I just had to make a present for Pa.

Gene made all his presents and wrapped them in comic paper, but he wouldn't tell me what they were. Mom usually knitted sweaters for each of us in the winter. She was always sewing. She took feed bags and made them into pillowcases or dishtowels. She took rags and made quilts. Mom made her dresses and jeans from store fabric.

Grandpa Phillips always worked in the basement making wooden toys for Gene and me or larger furniture items like tables and cabinets for Mom. This year, we were not allowed to go into the basement for any reason because he was making something special, and I didn't know what it was.

A week before Christmas, I still had no ideas for Pa's present. I finally decided to save my ten cents usually spent on the movies and get Pa a store-bought gift. I went to Kresge's Dime Store and looked at a razor and a pack of blades, but it cost twelve cents, and I only had a dime. I asked the man at the store if I could owe him two cents, but he said he couldn't do that. Pa used a brush and soap to shave with, but he always used the leftover soap that we used for bathing and washing the dishes. Mom made all of our soap from some kind of fat, but it smelled funny and didn't lather. For three cents, I could buy Pa some real shaving soap that smelled nice. I still couldn't see a movie at the Capitol Theater, but I had seven cents left for something else. I asked the man behind the store counter if he gift wrapped, but he only laughed at me. I didn't think it was funny.

Now I was all set for Christmas. On Saturday, Gene was going to the show, but I didn't have enough money. By some slice of luck, the Allis Theater had a matinee that day for only eight cents. The Allis wasn't as nice as the Capitol Theater, but it was still a show! Gene gave me a penny, and I went to the matinee. I couldn't wait to give out my gifts.

Buying a Christmas Tree

With just a week left before Christmas, Grandpa Phillips said it was time to look for a Christmas tree. We tramped through the woods near our home, but couldn't find a tree, so Pa, Gene, Grandpa Phillips, and I decided to drive to West Allis to buy a tree.

Most pine trees grew wild on farms and weren't grown specifically for Christmastime. We stopped at the tree stand we had bought from the year before. Most of the trees were over two dollars, and that was too costly for us, so we continued our search to a small lot next to a grocery store on 84th Street. The trees there cost less than two dollars but were scraggly and bent with missing branches or bare on one side. Additionally, they looked brown, but I guess all the trees looked like that.

We looked and looked until I found what I thought was the perfect tree. Grandpa Phillips called the others over to see it. Gene noticed it was missing a lot of branches and bare on one side, but Pa thought it would be a good tree if we added a few branches and put the bare side facing a corner. It was crooked and bent over a little, but Pa could put a wedge in the stand to make it look straight. It was as perfect as we could find. The tree lot owner wanted $1.50 for the tree, which was pretty high, but he wouldn't come down on the price. It was too good of a tree to pass up, so we took it. Pa paid two bits more for extra branches, and we tied the tree to the top of the car.

We drove straight home and showed the tree to the ladies. They agreed I had picked out the perfect tree, but we shouldn't have paid so much. Grandpa Phillips brought the tree to the garage and started drilling holes in the trunk. Then he placed six extra branches in the holes to make the tree look fuller. Now we had to wait until Christmas Eve before we could put it up. That was the very first tree I had ever picked out.

Christmas Eve

On Christmas Eve day, we brought our beautiful tree in from the garage and tried to set it in the tree stand. It was so twisted and crooked that we had to wedge it into the stand at an angle to make it look straight. One side was still bare and sparse, so Pa turned that side to the corner wall. We checked the string of lights because some of the wires were bare, and the bulbs had burned out. When we plugged the string in for the first time, we blew a fuse, and Pa and I had to go down to the basement to fix it. Sometimes Pa would screw in new fuses, and sparks would fly past his face and make me jump back. Fuses blew all the time, and replacing them was scary.

We had few ornaments but covered the tree with old tinsel that hid the spaces between the branches. It was the closest thing to a perfect tree that we ever had.

Gene and I practiced our lines for the Christmas Eve service at church that night. Every Christmas, I got sick to my stomach thinking about getting up in church to say my part of the program. I could always remember my lines, but I had terrible stage fright, and my mind would go blank. In school, I could never get up and talk. Some kids would go to the front and read their lines and start crying. Thank God, I never did that! Grandpa Phillips tried to tease me and told me that if I forgot my lines, I could say, "Santa comes once a year to bring whiskey, wine, and beer." He meant well, but it just made me more nervous. When we got to church, I was able to get up and say my lines, but I was sweating through them, even though the church was cold.

We stayed for hot chocolate and then went home to see if Santa had come. When we walked into the living room, the floor under the tree was loaded with gifts. Santa had come, just like I knew he would. I wondered if Gene would get anything after the Saint Nick's Day fiasco. Some of the gifts were wrapped in fancy paper, so we knew they were from Santa. Others were wrapped in the Sunday comic paper; those were from Mom, Pa, and Grandpa Phillips.

I opened my gift from Santa without tearing the paper so we could use it in the future. It was a large metal wind-up military tank. I wound it up, and it drove by itself across the floor. The Japanese soldier inside popped up with a gun and then went back into the tank. I had never seen anything like that before. Gene must have been somewhat good, too, because he got a "real" gun and holster and a real cowboy hat. Evelyn was older, so she got a pair of nylon hose. I felt sorry for her because you should get socks from your parents and shouldn't have to get them from Santa. Mom and Pa bought us socks, underwear, and flannel pajamas. And I got a box of six lead soldiers, and Gene got a record of Big Band music.

This was a big Christmas for us because we were so rich. Pa had a three-pound box of candy and nuts for all of us. Then we got the biggest surprise of all. Grandpa handed Gene a box wrapped in comic paper, and inside were two beautifully carved hunting knives and a wooden pistol. Gene was so excited because he loved Grandpa Phillips's woodwork. Then Grandpa Phillips brought out a great big box with my name on it. It was a wooden tool chest with small tools inside. I ended up using the chest for small toys and soldiers. We never expected that we would have such a big Christmas. I will never forget that Christmas because it was the last one we had with Grandpa Phillips.

Christmas Day

It was too cold that night to even get up to use the restroom in the bucket. I waited until Grandpa Phillips got up and started a fire in the kitchen's wood stove. Pa stocked the furnace, but it did little to warm the house against all the drafts. By 7 a.m., everyone was in the kitchen drinking coffee. Mom started to bake bread and cake for the big Christmas dinner. We had a small breakfast of corn flakes and toast with jelly before doing our chores.

The chicken coop was below freezing, and all the water was frozen. We filled water bottles with warm water and brought them out three or four times a day because the water froze within hours. We went back to the house with Grandpa Phillips for the biggest event of Christmas Day: checking the barrel of wine to see if it was ready. After fermenting only two months, it was still closer to grape juice, but we thought it was really strong wine. Grandpa Phillips would take a sip and hand the small glass to me. "Try this, Eddie. Do you think it is ready?"

Of course, I didn't know the difference between "ready" or "not ready," but I would roll the juice around in my mouth as Grandpa Phillips always did and then swallow. "I think it's ready, Grandpa."

"Okay, if you think it's ready," he said, "we'll have it with our Christmas dinner."

I don't remember dinners often being very special, but I felt really big when I was served wine with the adults. ✩✩

Chapter Six | 1938–1940
The In-Between Years

A Full House

We had a revolving door of relatives, friends, and neighbors in our house, always moving in and moving out. Before I could remember, Aunt Lily and Uncle John and my cousins Cate and Howie lived with us. Then Grandpa Phillips and Aunt Evelyn moved in. Then we got a new pastor at our church who needed a place to live while he finished seminary. Reverend Procter, a young man from out of state, moved in with us for about a year. He was like an older brother because he got into as much mischief as we did.

After he moved out, Aunt Rosa (Pa's sister) and her daughter, Shirley, and granddaughter moved in for about three years. Aunt Rosa's new friend, Walt Goodman, stayed for a while. My cousin, Mickey, lived with us for the next six years. Cousins Jack, Lorraine, and others stayed with us for months or a year. And on, and on, and on.

Missionaries to Japan

When I was six years old, I wanted to be a minister. Reverend Procter moved in with us during his year at seminary, and he became a full member of the family. We all worked in the fields together, did chores together, and had pillow fights. When we butchered the old hens, however, he refused to clean them or pluck the feathers. On Sunday mornings, he walked with our family to Sunday school, through the woods, past Spring Meadow, a small pond we often played in, and into the long cornfields that stretched from the meadow to the church. Sometimes, it would get so muddy that we would all pull up our pant legs to keep them clean. When we got to church, we'd all have to take our shoes off and wash them in a bucket of water.

In August, we had two national Japanese missionaries stay with us while they were at churches in Milwaukee. I had to sleep on the couch (which was mostly my permanent bed), and the three ministers shared one bedroom. The guests took the bed, and Reverend Procter slept on a cot. He was so tall that his ankles and feet hung over the end. I was small for my age, but the Japanese missionaries weren't much taller. They could fit on the cot with room spare.

One day, the missionaries and pastor were sitting on the porch talking about their mission work and how the Church was growing in Japan. From their talk, I naively gathered that they were the only two ministers in the country working with a Christian church. They said that most people in Japan had a different religion and were not friendly toward Christians.

Pa spoke up, telling the men how Gene and I made money by picking up pig metal and selling it to the junkyards. He heard it would eventually be shipped to Japan. Then he asked why Japan was buying all this iron. Neither missionary wanted to discuss the matter and tried to change the subject. Then one of them said things were changing in Japan. "No one dares ask questions," he said, "because officials come to our homes and inquire why we are asking questions, and that is none of our business." No one seemed to understand what they were talking about. Reverend Procter said he'd love to visit them in Japan, but the other responded, "You should not come to Japan. Things are changing. The government does not like foreign visitors."

"Well, then, when will you be coming back to America?" Reverend Procter asked. They didn't give an answer right away. Finally, they said, "We will probably never come back again." Everyone seemed uncomfortable, and nothing more was said about it. Then the missionaries talked about the wonderful meals they had with us.

Two years later, our church tried to reach out to the missionaries and bring them back to America again from Japan. The Japanese church we contacted replied that they no longer knew where the men were. After the war, our pastor contacted the church again in Japan and heard back from one of the members that the churches had been closed since the war started. The two missionaries had been taken into the army and both had died in action. Immediately after they went back to Japan, the missionaries sent me a handwritten letter in a small gold book that I kept for years, never knowing what they had written to me in Japanese. How sad that those two wonderful men had been forced to fight against us after being here and learning to love us.

The Horse Barn Fire

Every summer, the state fairgrounds had harness racing. For several months, the owners and trainers brought their horses to the park to train. After the race, they moved on to other states and tracks for the summer. Pa and I would go to the park every morning in our old Ford car and a trailer to pick up manure to mix with the soil.

Pa loved looking at the horses and talking to the trainers because as a young man he had worked at the Pabst Farms in Oconomowoc with the veterinarian caring for the farm's prize horses. He said it was the best job he'd ever had.

When we were finished loading the trailer, we spent the rest of the time looking at the horses. Pa could tell which had the best size, muscle tone, and stature to be a winning horse. We often watched the trainers on the track and stayed for some of the races.

The state fairgrounds had stalls on the north end next to the railroad tracks, so incoming livestock—horses, cows, and show stock—could be taken right to the stalls for the fair. The wood buildings were about 90 feet long, and there was one for cattle and another for racehorses.

Early one morning, about 2 a.m., we heard fire engines racing down 84th Street to the fairgrounds. Pa woke me up and drove to the park to see what was happening. We could see the flames thirty feet high coming from the horse barns. We parked the car on 84th Street and ran across the street to the barns to see several horses running from the flame-filled barns. They were screaming in a noise that I had never heard before. Several policemen ran after them and tried to stop them. Both barns were blazing, and dozens of workers and policemen were trying to save a few victims. Many of the animals died. By the time we left, half the neighbors were there. The scene was a nightmare I'll never forget. The barns were never rebuilt, and the harness races were never held there again.

Grandpa, My Partner

Grandpa Phillips was my closest friend. I followed him all day long, from working on the grape vines to taking care of the chickens. He would joke with me and tease me and always call me Eddie Lee. When I got into trouble, he would just chuckle and try to get me off the hook. He never got mad at me and always encouraged me to do whatever I wanted to do, but never to hurt anybody. I sucked raw eggs with him (and hated it!), helped him hide his whiskey from Mom, and even drank a little wine with him at night. He'd tell Mom, "I think Eddie has a cold coming on. He should have some wine." I never saw him mad other than at Grandfather Wendland, whom he called a crab-ass.

It was a warm, sunny Saturday morning. A local farmer had just plowed our field, and it had taken him all of the day before, walking behind his big work horse and plow. Grandpa Phillips was outside cultivating and raking a small area to plant sweet corn. By the time I ate breakfast and went outside, Grandpa Phillips was digging small holes to place the corn kernels into. He always put five kernels into each hole, and I always helped him.

He hadn't waited for me that day. My cousin, Russ, came over to help. He only lived a mile from the farm. Grandpa was giving Russ a hug for helping him plant. I heard him say that I was still sleeping, so he was glad to have such good help. I was hurt. I always did this with Grandpa Phillips. How could Grandpa Phillips let some cousin take my place? He was *my* grandpa.

Russ kept saying, "I love you, Grandpa." My grandpa wasn't Russ's grandpa. He was Gene's and mine.

I ran to hide in the chicken coop where no one would find me. I heard Grandpa Phillips calling for me, but I hid in the back of the feed room behind the barrels. He looked for me, but I wouldn't come out. I sat there until lunchtime and after Russ went home. At first, I wouldn't talk to Grandpa Phillips, but when he asked me to help him stake the tomato plants, I was happy. Grandpa Phillips realized once again that *I* was his helper, not some cousin of mine. I was his grandson, not Russ.

The next day, when we got home from church, my cousins Norman and Denny came over for the day. We finished a big chicken dinner and were sitting on the front porch when Grandpa Phillips asked Denny if he wanted to gather eggs with him. We went out to the coop to give the chickens fresh water, and then Grandpa Phillips gave Denny the basket for eggs. I tried to take it away from him, but Grandpa Phillips told me not to. "You do that every day, Eddie. Let Denny do it," he said. Then Denny grabbed Grandpa Phillips's arm and said, "I love you, Grandpa."

Why were all my cousins taking my grandpa? Let them get their own grandpas. I walked out of the coop to the woods to hide. Everyone wanted to take my Grandpa Phillips from me.

That evening, when Norman and Denny went home, Grandpa Phillips asked if I wanted to hear a story before I went to bed. I turned away and said, "No! Go tell it to my cousins, Russ and Denny. You like them better."

Grandpa Phillips tried to pick me up and throw me over his shoulder like he did every night, but I pulled away. "What's the matter, Eddie?" he asked. "Aren't we partners? We never fight."

"My cousins keep calling you 'Grandpa,'" I blurted out, "and you're not their grandpa! You're mine!"

"Eddie, Russ and Carla and Norman and Denny and you and Gene are all my grandchildren. Aunt Ella and your Uncle Richard are my children, just like your mother is my daughter. Their children—your cousins—are all my grandchildren. I'm their grandpa, too. Do you understand?"

"But you hug them like you hug me," I said.

"Eddie, I love all of you, but remember, you're my partner. Always remember, no one will ever replace you in my heart because you're my partner. Besides, you're the only one who knows where I hide my medicine bottles and that makes you special."

I didn't quite understand all these relationships, but I did know where his bottles were. ☆☆

Chapter Seven | 1940–1942
Difficult Times

Church in a Snowstorm

I always thought Sundays were special, and I liked going to church. On Sunday mornings, Mom, Gene, and I would get dressed early and walk a mile through the woods, over the tracks, past Spring Meadow, and across a cornfield to our little church. Mom and Aunt Ella were highly active in church ministries. Most of the congregation worked with the Salvation Army and other church groups. Sunday school never started until Mr. Ziglone came down the basement stairs and sat in his huge chair we called "the throne." He was about 300 pounds and, of course, walked very slowly. When I was young, I thought he was some kind of a priest. Mom was the Sunday school superintendent and would give a little talk to the thirty-some kids who came, and then we all went to our classes.

We often walked to church because Pa worked second shift at Harley Davidson, and he would sleep later and then meet us at church. Pa liked the old hymns at our church and was a great singer, but usually he would fall asleep during the sermon because he had worked so many hours. Mom used to poke him, "Pa, wake up! Pa, wake up!" He said he was just resting his eyes, but he would snore while he "rested" them. He told Reverend Procter once that he liked his sermon. Revered Procter thanked him and said, "Yeah, Herb, this is the first time you didn't interrupt me with your snoring!" Reverend Procter was our pastor for two years before he moved to a church in Princeton, Wisconsin.

One Sunday, we woke up to a very heavy snowstorm. The weather looked worse as we started getting dressed to leave, but we had walked through snowstorms many times, and none of us were concerned. Mom helped me get on my heavy snow pants with the straps that went over my shoulder. Before I started getting ready, I always went to the bathroom because heaven help me if I got all dressed up and then had to take my clothes all off. Next, Mom helped me get on my four-buckle boots that fit over my shoes. Once I had the heavy snowsuit on, I couldn't bend over to put the boots on by myself. Gene was lucky—he was older and didn't need snow pants.

I already had a sweater on and was ready for my woolen storm coat that weighed a ton. If you ever fell with all these clothes on, you couldn't get back up. Mom wrapped a scarf around my face because the snow was blowing hard. We were all ready, and I lumbered to the door, weighed down like an old mule carrying a 200-pound man. We walked out to the woods, and the wind didn't seem too bad. The snow was about six inches deep, but not drifted because the woods slowed down the wind.

Once we got out of the woods and onto 89th Street, the wind was stronger, and the drifts were high. Mom stopped for a moment but didn't say anything. I think she was deciding whether we should turn back. I was small and had a heart murmur, and she had had a heart attack the year before, not even forty years old. She decided we should go on, and we headed over the track past Spring Meadow. We stopped again at the tracks for a moment, as Mom debated again with herself if we should turn around. But since we only had a half-mile to walk through the cornfield, we continued. Mom was used to working hard with the produce and housework, but she didn't seem to have the same energy as she had in the past. She had often carried in loads of firewood from the garage and took care of the furnace when Pa was at work. This winter, though, Gene had to take over because she was so tired.

Mom started off into the field with Gene walking in her tracks and me lagging. The drifts were one or two feet high, and it was almost impossible to lift our legs with the weight of the snow. Mom stopped and asked how we were doing. Gene was almost as tall as Mom, but I was having trouble. She told Gene to tie his belt through his belt loops, and I was to hang onto it. We couldn't walk side by side, so Mom stomped in the snow to make tracks, and then Gene walked in her tracks, and I walked in Gene's tracks. We couldn't see anything ahead of us, and I didn't know how Mom could find her way.

Every few minutes, Mom would ask, "Eddie, are you hanging on? Eddie, are you okay? Gene, check Eddie." Her voice sounded frantic, and it scared me. Mom never seemed to get upset about anything. Then I heard her say to herself, "Thank God, there's the church." Once we got into the church hall, Mom sat down on the steps. Tears were coming down her cheeks, and I didn't know why she was crying. "Rose, are you okay?" asked the pastor.

"I'm just a little winded, and the snow makes my eyes water," she answered.

We made our way down to the basement, but Mr. Ziglone wasn't in his chair. Just a few kids showed up, and everyone had a story to tell about the storm. Just then, the outer door opened, and someone helped Mr. Ziglone down the stairs. He had walked three blocks in the storm because he knew we couldn't start without him.

The storm was so bad that they cancelled church for the first time since I had been going. Pa came to pick us up, but it took him a half-hour to drive two miles. Most of the roads were blocked with stalled cars. It was our worst memory of walking to church, but Gene and I both got gold stars for perfect attendance that year.

Saying Goodbye

I was seven-and-a-half years old, and still quite frail from the fever, but as long as I was with Grandpa Phillips, I was a happy boy. When Evelyn moved in with us, I moved in with Grandpa Phillips and shared his room with him, sleeping in the same bed together. He was always such fun and always stuck up for me no matter what I did. At night, he told me a story and carried me to bed. In the morning, I rushed to get dressed and hurry outside to help Grandpa Phillips with his chores. I was of little help to him, but he made me feel special and important.

In spring 1941, Pa bought 200 new chickens, so Grandpa Phillips and I cleaned out the brooder house and set up the heat lamps for our little babies. I loved to pick them up and rub them across my cheek. They were so soft and cute. Later in the day, Grandpa Phillips and I worked in the field, picking up rocks and throwing them onto the side of the road. Sometimes he would say, "Eddie, don't try to pick up that rock because it will hurt you. Some day you will grow up and be bigger and stronger than me, but first you have to grow a little."

Everyone else treated me like a weakling and said I would always be small and weak because something was wrong with my heart. But Grandpa Phillips said, "Don't believe them, Eddie. Someday, you'll outgrow your trouble and be the biggest man in the family. And don't forget that."

Then something happened. Grandpa Phillips was picking up a big rock and suddenly dropped to his knees. I thought he was just playing, but he didn't get up. His face turned white, and I got scared. "Don't worry, Eddie," he whispered, "I just had to get my breath."

That night, he didn't carry me to bed because he said his back was hurting him. Mom looked at him and asked if he was feeling okay. "Oh, just a little tired from picking rocks," he answered.

The next morning, I woke up before Grandpa Phillips. He just lay there sleeping. I had to go to school and never gave it a thought. Later that day, Grandpa Phillips came in from pushing the cultivator in the field and told Mom the sun was bothering him, and he wanted to cool off.

"Can you help me push the piano back, then?" she asked him. She had pulled the piano out from the wall to dust, but needed help pushing it back. It was on wheels but hard to maneuver on the floor rug. Grandpa Phillips took one side and Mom the other and pushed it back where it belonged. Grandpa turned to walk back to his chair when he fell to the floor. Mom couldn't pick him up, so she called Grandfather Wendland to come downstairs to help her get Grandpa Phillips into bed.

When I got home from school, the doctor had been there, and Grandpa Phillips was in bed. The doctor said Grandpa Phillips had had a slight heart attack and would have to get a lot of rest. Most families at the time didn't have money or insurance to go to a hospital, so illnesses were treated at home. Grandpa Phillips joked with me that now we both had lazy hearts and would have to take it easy, but we were tough and would get over it.

The next morning, May 3, I woke up, but Grandpa Phillips was still sleeping in bed beside me. Mom came in to check him and told me I should dress in the kitchen and let Grandpa Phillips sleep. I wanted to say goodbye to him before I went to school, but Mom said I should let him sleep. She said she would tell him when he woke up. Mom seemed upset, but just said, "Don't worry, honey, it will be okay."

When I got back home from school, Mom told me Grandpa Phillips had gone to visit Grandma and would be gone for a long time.

My best friend was gone. He had died in bed next to me while we both slept.

The Lake

The summer of 1941 was a warm one. When Grandpa Phillips passed away, we had to take over his chores and the responsibilities of the chickens that he always tended to. We never realized how much work he had until it shifted onto our shoulders.

In August, Pa said he and his sister, my Aunt Rosa (not to be confused with my mom, Rose), had rented a cottage on Lake Sinissippi. He would stay home during the week while we were at the cottage, and then he would join us on the weekends. We had never been to this lake before or a cottage during the summer because we always had work to do, but Pa said some sort of sickness that hurt kids was making its way around, and he wanted us out of the city. The sickness was polio.

We had driven for about an hour when we reached Hustisford, driving around the town until we came to a great big house on the top of the hill above the lake. The lake was as blue as the sky and looked large to me. A long pier ran into the water, and a small rowboat and a little sailboat were pulled up onto the shore. The house was old with a lot of rooms. Only two rooms had actual beds, and the others only had small cots and little furniture. The outhouse was only a few feet away from the house, so that was nice. Even still, I could see that Mom was not happy with the place.

Uncle Stan came out to join us with Aunt Rosa, my cousin Shirley, and her friend Gloria. The two girls were both seventeen and very silly. It took all of us several hours to clean the house before it was livable. But once we were done, we headed to the lake for a swim.

Since my four-year-old near-drowning experience, I had been afraid of the water, and this lake was no different. But Pa said it was so shallow that we could wade halfway across the lake.

The next day, we drove into Hustisford to pick up groceries, and then that night, Uncle Stan and Pa left to go back to their homes for a week of work.

Our first few days at the lake were all the same: we spent every moment swimming (or wading for me!) and rowing around the shoreline to check out the houses. We didn't have the car, so we had to walk to the village if we needed anything. It was about a mile away, and we had great fun walking and singing as we went with Shirley and Gloria. Their favorite songs were "Three Little Fishies" and "Mairzy Doats." I can't remember the rest, but they were fun.

The village's downtown was three blocks long. It had a small grocery store, butcher shop, drug and hardware stores, and several other little shops. The girls shopped while Gene and I explored the river and the big dam on the Rock River that formed the lake. Several teenagers were walking back and forth across the dam. It was about thirty feet high, and the lake water collected to the very top of the other side of the dam. As the teens walked toward us, they joked and poked fun at us "city kids," daring us to walk the dam.

Gene was almost twelve and didn't take well to people daring him to do things. Even then, he didn't show fear. We walked up to the dam, and it looked scary. We could see big carp swimming in the shallow water around the big dam. Gene made a rash decision and determined he would risk it. I didn't want him to. It was so high, and the dam was slippery from the water splashing about it. But those teens wouldn't stop taunting us. Gene's chin grew stiffer and stiffer listening to them. He jumped up and started climbing. I felt I should follow, but I was scared and shouted to Gene to come back down. I was too small.

Gene strolled across the dam like he was walking down a garden path. Then he took some stones out of his pocket and threw them down at the fish way below. I could see the teens were surprised and impressed. Gene could always put on a good show. He walked over as cocky as he could and let them know we weren't city kids. We had a ranch outside of Milwaukee, he told them, and had to get away before we brought the cattle in for finishing. I didn't know what that meant, but I sure was proud to be with Gene that day. He never backed down.

We didn't tell anyone about Gene walking the dam, or Mom would have had a heart attack. But I know Pa would have said, "Good for you, Gene. Never back down, because doing so will only become a habit."

Danger on the High Seas

We had been at the cottage in Hustisford for a week. The weather was beautiful, the lake was perfect, and the fishing was great. Pa came for the weekend and bought Gene and me new extension cane fishing poles. They came apart in three sections, and boy, did we think we were rich!

A bakery truck came to the cottage twice a week, and Aunt Rosa bought us all cherry pies. I loved cherry pie. I could eat as much as I wanted, so one day, I ate a whole pie by myself. I got crazy sick and never wanted to see cherry pie again.

Shirley and Gloria were always laughing and getting themselves into mischief. One day, they caught a snapping turtle and put it in the house. When Aunt Rosa opened the door, the turtle snapped its head out and tried to bite her. She came running out screaming; she was so mad. Every day, the girls wanted to take the sailboat out. It was a small boat with a pole and a canvas. I had never seen a sailboat like it before, and Aunt Rosa always told them no. "You don't know anything about sailboats," she insisted, "and you'll drown." Personally, I didn't know who would miss them. They were always causing trouble and making Aunt Rosa mad.

Finally, one calm morning, Aunt Rosa gave into their pleas in hopes they would shut up. Gene and the girls carried the boat to the water, and they connected the sail with some kind of rope. It was only big enough for two, so the girls hopped in and used a paddle to get offshore. Then they lifted the sail. The boat didn't even move. The wind was calm. They brought it out the next day after lunch for another go. Everybody was excited because the wind had picked up and the boat actually sailed. It looked like fun. Then I wished I could sail. The girls seemed to skim over the lake whenever the wind came up.

An island lay in the lake about a hundred yards from the cottage, and the two girls had almost reached it. The wind picked up unexpectedly, and the lake started churning. Aunt Rosa and Mom began to yell at the kids to come home, but they were too far to hear. The little boat seemed to be spinning around in the wind, and we could hear the girls screaming. Gene ran over to the neighbors to see if they could help. They had a big boat with a motor. Mom called the Sheriff's Department for help. Before the sheriff arrived, the men next door, Mel and Warren, had started their motorboat and took off over the lake toward the girls. The sailboat had capsized onto its side, and both Gloria and Shirley were hanging on and crying, "Help! We'll drown!" We watched from the shoreline but couldn't do anything.

Mel and Warren got to the capsized boat and pulled the girls into their boat. The sheriff arrived and looked out toward the motorboat heading back with the crying girls and the disabled boat. Mel suddenly stopped the boat, climbed out, and stood up, spotting the depth of the lake at four feet. He up-righted the sailboat and towed the boat home.

Once on shore, Mel pulled the sailboat onto the beach and said with exasperation, "Next time your boat turns over, just walk home." The deepest spot between our cottage and the island turned out to be only five feet deep. The girls didn't think that was funny.

A week later, the Hustisford newspaper published a front-page story about the two teenage girls who were rescued on the lake. They were the talk of the town. When Gloria got home at the end of the summer, she took swimming lessons. Cousin Shirley swore she would never get into a boat again. She ended up marrying a sailor and bought a home in Oconomowoc on the lake.

The Car Accident

It was a cool fall day, and Pa was making French toast for breakfast. We had a stovetop grill that fit over all four burners, and Pa could make as many as eight pieces of "amarita" (what he called French toast) at a time. We could eat them as fast as he could make them. Evelyn and Glen got married and moved away to Texas. For the first time, we lived alone with only Grandfather Wendland and Margaret upstairs. Pa had planned to drive to Menomonee Valley to pick up hardware. In the Valley was a charming little town called Wauwatosa. It had a little river that meandered through its center. Sometimes we went there with a lunch and fishing poles and spent the day. The Number 10 streetcar started there and ran across the Valley to downtown Milwaukee. It was our favorite train because it ran two miles above the treetops and buildings, and we could see for miles around. People came from all over just to ride the Number 10.

We went to the lumberyard first and picked up the hardware and then got out to look at the river and see if anybody had caught any fish. The scenery was beautiful, but the fishing was lousy. We drove up the road and stopped in front of Wauwatosa High School, where I wanted to go to school one day.

We pulled up to a stop sign when suddenly the car lurched

forward with a horrible crashing sound as someone from behind hit us. Gene and I flew off our seats onto the floor. I heard Pa screaming, "Rose! Rose! Can you hear me?"

As we looked up, we saw that Mom had flown through the front window, and her face was a mask of blood. Pa leaned over and tried to release her from the shards of glass, but it seemed impossible to move her without cutting up her face. She didn't make a sound, and Gene and I both screamed, "Our mom is dead." A man reached in front of the passenger side and helped Pa release her. Someone called the county hospital located a short distance away, and they lifted Mom out of the car, but she never made a sound.

The man who helped take Mom out of the car was the driver of the gravel truck who had hit us. Pa had to wait for the police to come after the ambulance. The dump truck driver claimed he was driving at city speed but didn't pay attention to the fact that we had stopped for a sign. His truck was loaded with several tons of gravel, and he was driving to a construction site. He said he had tried applying his brakes, but they didn't work. The police double-checked his brakes, deciding the man had been driving too fast and didn't stop for us or the sign. The police didn't arrest him, but he had to go to court.

The back end of our car was caved in, and the windshield was out on the car's passenger side. The police offered to drive us to the hospital, but Pa drove us over since our car still ran. Mom had been rushed into surgery, but the worst of her injuries was a severe concussion. We didn't see her for several hours, but when we did, the staff said she was sleeping. I think she hadn't woken up from the accident.

Two weeks later, we brought Mom home, but she could barely talk and was confined to bed. We could talk to her, but she didn't seem to know who we were. Pa had to hire a full-time nurse to take care of Mom and us when he went to work. All the expenses were paid for by the trucking company of the man who hit us. I don't remember the nurse's name, but she was an older lady—maybe fifty—and nasty.

At that time, Gene was in the Boy Scouts and often stayed at his best friend, Donnie's house. Later, they both raised homing pigeons and sent notes back and forth every day. Donnie took up flying at the age of sixteen and died in a plane crash a year later. Gene never got over it. He always hated the farm and our lifestyle, and I think he resented our parents for it. He couldn't wait to run away from home, and he tried several times. One time, Mom found a note that he was running away and ran three blocks to try to catch him at the bus stop. Gene sold all his pigeons and never had a pet again. By the time he was eighteen, he had gone on the road with a big band.

It took several weeks before Mom could talk and recognize us. We kept the nurse for about two months, but I was happy to see her go. She would often pinch me if I didn't do what she said, and she combed my hair so hard in the morning it would penetrate my scalp and draw blood. Mom never recovered fully from the accident. Before, she was always very calm and never fretted about where we were or what we were doing. After the accident, she was always afraid something was going to happen to us. She always thought we were going to get hurt. But she did get her strength back, and she went on to do great things.

Jail Time

When I was eight years old, our entertainment came mostly from the radio, weekly movies, and comic books. We could seldom afford ten cents for comic books, so we would trade baseball cards, marbles, or anything else of value for a comic book. Gene and I had to wash the dishes after dinner twice a week. He hated doing them, so I offered to take his turn if he gave me a comic book. I had already picked the one I wanted before I offered a negotiation.

After several years of living on the farm, we expanded our raspberry patch to over a half-acre and the strawberries and currants. Mom would pay us three cents for every quart of berries we picked. We were picking over thirty quarts a day altogether, and I was making nine cents for my work. Some weeks, I made as much as fifty cents in all. With all that wealth, I decided to buy two brand-new comic books.

I went to Sam's Drugstore on Greenfield and spent over twenty minutes looking through *Superman* comic books. I finally decided on two and took them to the counter. Sam put them into a bag and asked me for ten cents. I knew they were ten cents *each*, but he had only asked for a dime. I didn't say a word and gave him five pennies and a nickel. When I got outside the store, I knew he had made a mistake, and I knew I had made a mistake. I should have gone back in but didn't want to give him the other dime. Deep down, I knew it was stealing, but I reconciled with the fact that it had been his fault, not mine. I ran home as happy as a lark because I had two *Superman* comics and had saved a dime.

After I went to our room, I thought through the situation again. Maybe he would realize his mistake, and I would get arrested. What would my mom say if I went to jail? No one in the family had ever gone to jail other than my grandpa after getting into a fight leaving Kovichock's Bar. But he came home the same day. I wondered if God was watching.

I had a terrible night. I didn't tell anybody, and I wished Grandpa Phillips was there. He would have told me what I should do. The next morning, we had breakfast, and Mom asked me why I was so quiet. "Are you feeling okay, Eddie?" I didn't answer her because she wouldn't want to talk to me once she knew I was going to jail.

After breakfast, I took the books and ran down to Sam's

Drugstore to give them back or pay the extra dime. *What if he calls the police? What if he calls Mom?* I wished I were dead, and then I wouldn't have to face him.

When I walked into the store, Sam was behind the counter. I put the two books down and started blabbering. "I stole one of your books. Please don't call my parents. I don't want to go to jail! I didn't mean to do it. I have the extra dime. Oh, and I didn't cut off the top of the page, honest. It was like that—honest." Then the tears came and wouldn't stop. Sam hadn't said a word. I just kept talking.

Finally, he told me to calm down. "I know you didn't cut off the top of the page. I did that," he said. "We do that when we consider the books old. Then we mark them down half-price. The books you bought were only a nickel, so it only cost a dime for the two of them. Do you understand? You didn't steal them. That's what the price was. Do you understand, Eddie? You didn't steal anything."

I stood there for a long time, finally finishing my cry. "I thought I stole them."

"No, Eddie, you didn't steal them." He put the books into another bag. "And Eddie, if you were my son, I would be proud of you. Now, go home and enjoy your new books." ☆

Chapter Eight | 1942
Mikey, Who Didn't Fight

Mikey Moves In

Several years after Evelyn got married and moved out, Pa offered to help Aunt Marion move. Early Saturday morning, we drove to Milwaukee's north side, where Aunt Marion lived in an upper flat. When we got to the apartment, Uncle Lester wasn't there to help move. As I later found out, they were getting a divorce, so she had to move in with a friend. Kids were never told anything that adults were doing, so we had no idea what was planned.

My cousin Mikey and I played on the winding stairway as Mom and Pa carried things down to the trailer. After they finished, Mikey said goodbye to his mother and came home with us. We didn't know at the time, but Mom and Pa were going to raise Mikey because his dad didn't want him, and Aunt Marion couldn't take care of him now. Mikey was two years younger than I, so now I was like his older brother. I would end up protecting him for six years because Mikey had a habit of attracting fights that he couldn't finish.

Gene and I were taught to be neat from the time we were very young. When we came home from church or school, we hung up our clothes and put on play clothes. If we had our toys out, we put them away when we were done. We made our beds, washed dishes, and even did the laundry several times. Every day we had our chores to do before we went to school. We never used Pa's tools without his permission, and we always put them away when we were done.

One day we all came home from school and found our toys thrown all over the yard and in the fields. Mikey started screaming and crying that someone had thrown all his toys away. I didn't have many toys, but Mikey had brought a lot of toys with him. The day before, Pa had asked where his tools were, and Mikey said he had been building something and just left them where he was working. Today, Pa told Mikey he played with his toys in the yard and forgot he left them out in the fields. He had really taken all the toys and thrown them all over the yard, but he meant to teach Mikey a lesson. It took us three hours to find most of the toys, and some we never found. Lesson number one.

Mikey's Second Lesson

One day while Mikey and I played Monopoly, we got into a fight. Pa came and asked what the problem was. Mikey told Pa I was cheating, and Pa seemed to be very sympathetic. He didn't want us to be unhappy and fighting, so he picked up the game and all the money and pieces, walked down to the basement, and threw everything in the furnace. "Now," he said, "this won't bother you anymore."

Mikey's Third Lesson

We were playing marbles, and Mikey accused me of cheating again. Pa came in and found we were unhappy playing marbles, so he solved our problem. We had over 300 of our best marbles and shooters in a box. Pa picked up all the marbles, put them in the box, carried them outside, and threw them down the road. We had very real fights after that.

Mikey's problem was that he had a smart mouth and a surly attitude and made a lot of enemies. I never really liked to fight, but he got used to me getting him out of trouble. In fact, he threatened everybody that if they picked on him, his cousin would beat them up. For the next six years, I fought his battles but never had any of my own. After he moved out, I never fought with anybody.

One day when I was coming out of Genkee's Downtown Grocery, I saw four kids beating up another kid on the next block. As I got closer, I saw that it was Mikey, and he was being beaten up by kids from 88th Street. We had never had a problem with those kids. In fact, sometimes they helped me when I had conflicts with the Walker kids.

I ran up and jumped on two of the kids, and they went down. One kid got off Mikey, and we exchanged blows. Mikey snuck away, as usual, and left me to fight. We did a little more pushing, shoving, and knocking down, but then I realized that I liked these guys. Jerry, my friend from school, was part of that street and was one of my close friends. We sat down after we all got tired, and I asked why they were after Mikey. No one remembered. They just knew they didn't like him, and he had smarted off. Then the guys gave me some good advice: "Stop fighting his battles."

We all went away friends.

Being a Big Brother

When my cousin, Mikey, moved in with us, my life changed. I was no longer considered the baby of the family. Now I was a big brother, and I was fully responsible for my little brother. If anyone picked on Mikey, they had to deal with me. Mikey and I got along well, but if we argued, I was bigger, so I always won.

Mikey swore all the time, and our family never swore. Mom tried to wash his mouth out with soap, but it turned out that Mikey liked the taste of soap. In fact, he would chew on soap, his favorites being the Ivory and Lux soaps, so Mom never bought the soaps he liked.

Mikey and I did some stupid things—I usually thought them up. One day, we went to the movies to watch a double feature of *Superman*. I noticed that Superman would always run first, jump into the air with his arms stretched out and his cape behind him, and then he would fly. I thought his cape kept him airborne. So I decided that if we ran off the top of the garage and did the same things Superman had done, we, too, could fly.

For some reason, Mikey didn't like the idea when I tried to convince him that he needed to go first. There was a big pile of straw at one end of the garage, and if Mikey didn't fly, he would only fall into the nice soft straw. We both put on capes, and Mikey ran across the three-car garage, stretched out his arms, and flew like a bird—for ten feet!

He took a sudden dive right into the straw pile. He remembered all his swear words and used them all. Upon watching him, I thought it best that I did not try to fly next. I may have been wrong about our capabilities.

Pet Day

Today was the day! Every spring, the week before we got out of school, we had pet day. Anyone could bring his or her pet to school, so long as the pet was small and friendly. Gene wasn't going to take anything because he had given away most of his pigeons.

Mom asked if Mikey and I were taking a chicken or one of the cats. We only had a few chickens left for our own eggs, and none of them was my pet. Anyway, I had taken a chicken for the previous three years, so I decided to take Peanuts instead.

Peanuts was the smallest of our three pigs. He was very tame. Mikey and I spent a lot of time playing with him, so he was used to people. Rufus and Peewee were larger pigs and not friendly.

"Don't be silly," Mom said. "You can't take a pig to school."

"A lot of kids take their pet rats or mice, and one kid had a guinea pig," I protested. "Why can't I take my pet pig?"

"First of all, a pig is not a pet. Did you ever go to anyone's house who had a pet pig? It's a farm animal!"

"Well, so is a chicken or a duck!" I couldn't see the difference.

After a while, I gave up the fight and got ready for school. Gene walked ahead with his friends, and Mikey and I went to the machine shed to pick out one of the roosters. Big Red was the king of the coop, and although a pretty bird, he was mean. We both tried to catch him, but after a few minutes, he was chasing us around the coop. He was an ugly-tempered chicken, and we decided not to fool with him. Not when we really could, just maybe, take a very friendly little pig.

When we entered the pigpen, the three pigs came running over thinking we had food for them. Pigs are so much friendlier than roosters. I told Mikey to keep quiet because I didn't want Mom to hear us. Pa was still sleeping after working second shift, but Mom would be mad that we didn't listen to her.

I tied up a rope to use as a collar, so all we had to do was put it around Peanuts' neck and walk him to school. He sat still as we put the collar on, and then I walked him out of the pen. As I tried to close the latch on the door, Peanuts slipped out of his noose and started running around like he wanted to play. Mikey grabbed his tail but got pulled down.

Peanuts started running through the raspberry patch toward the woods. By this time, kids were walking by with their pets, and one of the twins was bringing his dog for the pet show. The dog broke loose and started after the pig. Vincent's cat got excited and jumped out of his arms and took off. This was not going according to plan.

When all the kids started screaming, Pa woke up and came outside to see what the ruckus was about. The pig ran through the woods to 89th Street, across the street, and up the alley halfway to school. Mikey thought he knew the way and was in a hurry. One of the homeowners came out and screamed that a pig was ruining her garden and tried to hit Peanuts with a broom. Women always used a broom as a weapon of choice.

By this time, half the neighborhood, their dogs, and Pa were chasing Peanuts. The sheriff was called and told a rabid pig was running through yards. At that point, Peanuts *was* foaming at the mouth from running so long.

We finally caught up with Peanuts in Mrs. Stanton's yard, which was fenced. Unfortunately, she was the fifth-grade teacher who had no sense of humor. And I happened to be in her class at that time.

Pa caught the pig and tied his front legs. He carried Peanuts to the car, and Mikey and I held him in the back seat. When we got home, Mom wasn't in a good mood. Mikey and I ended up taking the nasty rooster, who got loose and hurt some of the kids in the class.

It wasn't a good day.

The Fire

Charlie T. was a boy from the neighborhood who always caused trouble. He lived just two blocks from us on Walker Street. Walker Street had its group of kids, the largest in the area. If you had a problem with anyone from Walker Street, you had to take on the whole group because they stuck together. Understand these were really nice kids, and we all got along well, but we had several social disagreements. The 88th Street kids had their gang, and so did the Schlinger Avenue kids. I lived on McMyron Street, and we only had six to eight kids in our group, and half of them were useless in a fight. When the bank sold off part of our farm and built new homes across from us, Vince moved in, and he was a fighter. He was short, like his father, and one year younger than me, but he was a fighter. I ran our neighborhood group, and Vince was the guy who always watched my back.

One day, I was coming home from school when I heard someone screaming in the woods. It didn't sound like anyone playing, but someone in real trouble. I started running down the path and through the woods when I noticed smoke at the top of the hill. We always worried about fires this time of the year because the woods could go up in flames.

I came to the clearing and saw Mikey tied to a tree surrounded by fire and Charlie T. throwing wood on the fire. It had rained the night before, so the leaves and twigs were burning slowly. When Charlie saw me coming, he started running down the hill. I tried to kick the fire from Mikey's feet. I left Mikey screaming and crying and went after Charlie. He had a head start, so I went back to get Mikey. He was screaming and swearing that he was going to get Charlie.

Charlie told the Walker kids that I had tried to beat him up and chased him all the way home. He said I threatened him and would stop him from having access to the woods. Part of this was true—I had chased him home—but he forgot to tell the gang he had tied Mikey to a tree and was going to sacrifice him to the gods. If they had known this, they wouldn't have come after me. Charlie was known for starting fires all over town. All the Walker kids planned to come up later and teach us a lesson.

We could only get the twins (they were useless), Dickie, Mikey, and Vince together in our gang. We waited at the top of the woods where Charlie had tried to toast Mikey. Vince was my best fighter and would watch my back so they didn't get me down. Sometimes we called my cousin Denny to come over and equalize the odds, but it was too late for that this time. Denny could take on three kids by himself. He was much tougher than I, but thank God, we never fought each other. Denny was a very easygoing guy.

We waited for about fifteen minutes, but I knew the Walker kids would be coming. Just then, we heard them screaming as they swarmed up the hill looking for revenge. I thought Patton's Fifth Army was attacking us. I didn't know they even had that many kids in their neighborhood. We were as good as dead.

Mikey took one look at the gang, and he was gone. The kids came at me like a Sherman tank. Vince had a full-time job trying to keep them off my back, but we were overwhelmed in less than ten minutes. For all the noise, nobody got hurt, nor was that allowed. It was just fun, but they were disappointed with our trepid response. I told them what Charlie had done. They thought it would be great fun to get all the kids together and give us a little scare. Charlie may have been a troublemaker, but he was smart enough to stay out of my way. For the next two weeks, I could not find that kid. In the meantime, he was telling everyone he was going to get back at me; that I had better watch out because it was going to be big; and that I would pay for this. I knew he would never take me on, but I kept a watchful eye on Mikey. I thought he was the target.

Sundays were always family days. We dressed up and went to Sunday school and church and then came home, and Mom would make a big chicken dinner with a pie or cake for dessert. Sometimes we would go to a lake and go fishing for the afternoon or just take a drive. Sunday night, we always stopped for hot ham and rolls or stayed home and played cards or games. Sometimes we went to the Church of the Open Door on 27th Street. Or if we had a little money, we went to see a movie at the Grace or National theaters where we could park on a hill. Just in case the car didn't start, we could push it down the hill.

It was a beautiful fall day, and the trees were dropping their leaves. The weather had been very dry. We all sat down for our big chicken dinner when someone saw smoke coming out of the woods. This was always a concern since we had several fires in the woods from campers or lightning storms. Thank God none of them had ever spread.

Two houses were built on the edge of the woods with a large field of grass next to the city houses. If that went up in flames, it would be almost impossible to stop. Some farmers in the township would burn off their fields for planting, and then it would get out of control, and the houses or barns would catch fire.

We dropped our food and ran outside to find the south end of the woods on fire near the chicken coops. We had over 300 layers and a number of roosting chickens in our coop. If it caught fire, they would all be toasted. Gene had several prize pigeons that he was going to show next spring at the fair. We had gone through similar fires before, so everyone knew their jobs.

Mom began to fill the buckets with water. Pa ran out to the fire with axes and shovels while Gene and I grabbed a pile of burlap bags and followed him. Mom called several neighbors that would be most affected, and Mr. Shanahan was there in minutes with five of his six girls to help. We always called the neighbors first because the volunteer fire department usually didn't come until after the fire was out. One of our neighbors had a house fire, and the fire department came just in time to watch the building fall into ashes.

Our biggest concern was taking care of our buildings, but a fire in the woods in the fall could be a disaster for everyone in the area. In addition, the south end was near the prairie grass fields, and a fire there could spread as fast as you could run.

By the time Pa got into the woods, several other men were there with axes, shovels, and tools to chop down the underbrush that burned very quickly. Mom and the kids soaked down burlap bags for pounding on the ground fires. Within ten minutes, the whole neighborhood was helping us fight the fire. A dozen kids and women carried water to the fighters. They soaked down the sides of the coops so the sparks wouldn't start the roof on fire. It took us over an hour to get the fire under control. Sure enough, the fire department came too late with water tanks and saturated the area with water.

Gene had moved all the chickens out of the buildings into the yard, as well as his prized pigeons to the garage, where he put them in cages. Everyone sat on the ground dead tired. Mom and some of the ladies brought out soda and beer for everyone, and I don't think anyone left for an hour or two. Everyone laughed and joked about how funny we must have looked running around like chickens with their heads cut off.

The fire department asked how the fire had started, but no one had any idea. There were no campers in the woods, and most people were at church or home on Sunday. Then I told them about Charlie T. He had started fires before in the area, but they never amounted to anything. When everyone heard about what happened to Mikey, though, they were very suspicious. The sheriff knew where Charlie lived because the whole family caused trouble.

"But did anybody see him?" the sheriff asked. He had everyone search the area for a gas can or any evidence.

The sheriff went to Charlie's house, and his parents said he had been home. They were shocked to hear there had been a fire in the woods. They hadn't heard a thing. They lived right across the street from the field of grass that was on fire, but they hadn't heard a thing. Every other neighbor nearby was helping to stop the fire.

The sheriff suspected it had been Charlie and so did the whole neighborhood, but we couldn't prove it. The sheriff told Pa that he couldn't do anything until they had evidence, but he said a firebug usually made two mistakes: he liked to stay and watch the fire, and he liked to brag to someone that he had done it. Until then, we waited.

About a week later, Charlie was bragging to some friends that he had tried to burn down Wendland's chicken coop and kill all their stupid birds, and the next time he tried, he would succeed. When word got back to us, we kids decided we would keep watch of the coop after school. We had a hiding place in the grapevines where no one could see us. Every day after school, Vince, Mikey, and I would sit out there and wait. After several days, we gave up and thought it was just a bluff.

A week later, Mr. Schultz, who lived down on the next corner across from Charlie, called and said he saw Charlie carrying a gallon milk bottle past his house toward the woods. Pa called the sheriff, who lived a few blocks away, and he came right over. They decided to walk into the woods where they couldn't be seen and find out what Charlie was doing. Charlie was so focused on what he was doing that the sheriff surprised him when he asked what he was up to. Charlie said he was looking at the fire damage. The sheriff checked the milk bottle, and it was filled with gas.

The Champ

Gene grabbed his bat and glove and headed out the door. I knew the neighborhood was having a baseball game, but I hadn't been invited. I was the worse ballplayer on the block, and no one wanted me on their team. When the captains chose the boys for their teams, I was always the last one left, and they'd always tell me to go home. It was 1942, and everyone wanted to grow up to play for the Chicago Cubs. We didn't have a major league team in Milwaukee, so we were Cubbie fans. Every afternoon, I listened to the Cubs. Everyone liked Andy Pafko and how he'd run and dive into the turf to catch a fly ball, even if it was a pop-up. We didn't know it then, but Andy would someday join the major league team the Milwaukee Braves. That was a special treat because Andy came from Boyceville, Wisconsin.

Gene was the best player in the neighborhood, and I knew he was ashamed of me. So I made up my mind that I'd practice every day. I'd show them. Every day, I would throw the ball straight up into the air and catch it. Then I talked Mikey into chasing the ball when we played Peggy—when you'd throw the ball into the air and hit it with a bat. The first couple of days Mikey just sat on the ground, waiting for me to hit anything. After several days, I could hit the ball almost every time. Then I had to bribe him to chase the ball.

Every morning before going to school, I practiced throwing the ball at a small square on the machine shed next to the house. Pa worked nights and would scream at me for waking him up. It took me several weeks before I was ready, but I finally believed a new star had been born.

The next Saturday, a big game was planned across from the outhouse that used to be part of the farm. The two team captains selected their teams, but still, no one picked me. One team was short a player, so they took me along. They put me in right field and hoped no one would hit the ball to me. Believe me, every player on the other team tried. Finally, a ground ball came my way. I ran after it and almost tripped. I could hear the moans of my teammates. I scooped up the ball and threw it for the first out. No one said a word—like it never happened.

It was the ninth inning, and we were down by two. We had two men on base with two outs. It was my turn to bat, but they tried to put in a pinch hitter. It became a big fight, but the umpire wouldn't allow it. I missed the first two swings, and everyone knew we were dead. I lowered my stance, spread my legs, and swung at the bad pitch. It was a ground ball, past the second base into right field. The kid bobbled the ball and threw it home. It was too late, though. Both runs ahead of me came in, and I picked up my pace for the last point, and we won the game.

Gene was the second runner to come in, so they picked him up and carried him around cheering. No one came over to say anything to me. This was not the movie ending I had expected. I started walking off the field when Gene came over and gave me a big hug. "I'm proud of you, Eddie," he said. "You knew that meant more to me."

The next week, Gene grabbed his bat and started walking out the door. He turned around and called out, "C'mon, Champ! The Wendlands have to win another game!" ☆☆

Chapter Nine | 1942–1945
The Great War

The German Bund Camps

As early as 1938, Adolf Hitler began promoting his philosophies in America. During that year, I would sit on my bed, and Grandpa Phillips and Grandfather Wendland would pull up their kitchen chairs a few feet from the shortwave radio. Adolf Hitler would make his weekly speech in Germany, and my grandpas would hang on every word. With Grandfather Wendland's military background in Germany, he loved to listen to Hitler and his "Super Race." He also thought it would be wise to get rid of those "damn Jews," he said. "All they do is suck money out of the country." Grandfather Wendland seemed to say the same thing every time his leader would talk.

Grandpa Phillips moved to Germany from Wales as a small boy, and his family had a little department store in Munich. He married Grandma, and they moved to the United States in the 1890s, where Grandpa Phillips worked as a silversmith. He invented the backing used for mirrors but was so financially broke at the time that he sold the patent for $100.

Both men were well-educated and very smart. But Grandpa Phillips was partially Jewish and hated Hitler and all that he stood for. Grandpa Phillips said that Hitler just wanted war, and he would get it. After a short time, Grandpa Phillips and Grandfather Wendland would start screaming at each other, and Mom or Evelyn would pull me out of the room before the fist fight started. The two men hated each other, and several times when they went drinking at the bar on 84th Street, they would get into fist fights, and the police would have to be called.

Grandfather Wendland heard about the rise of Bund Camps in America for children of German descent in 1938. He would have given anything for Gene and me to belong to one, but our parents had no use for the Hitler youth group. Young boys went to these camps on weekends and several weeks in the summer to be indoctrinated into the German American party. They had parades, learned how to march, had physical training, and swore allegiance to Germany. There was a large camp in the Milwaukee area because the city had a large second-generation German population. There was another camp in Waukesha County. Pa drove by it one time and showed us where it was, but we didn't see any activity.

Rumors of War

A big Christian rally was to be held in the auditorium of downtown Milwaukee. Mom, Aunt Ella, and Aunt Marion had planned to go together. They all met at Ella's house and took the streetcar downtown. At that time, very few women drove. In fact, some families didn't even have a car. The auditorium was packed full, with thousands of people—mostly women—for the big rally.

The program started off with the usual Christian songs, led by a well-known church leader and large choir. Several speakers prayed and read the scriptures, and then the main speaker walked on the stage. This was to be a Christian revival, and the crowd was quiet in anticipation. The speaker was a middle-aged handsome man with a German accent. He read a few verses from scripture and offered several touching stories of people who were saved. Then he started talking about how Christians all over the world should work together for world peace and how some nations, like

Germany, were trying to build a new world order of peace and prosperity. Aunt Marion became a little irritated at what this man was calling a sermon. She looked at her sisters for their opinions.

In the middle of the "sermon," a second flag with a swastika was draped down next to the American flag. At that moment, Aunt Marion jumped up and hollered as loud as she could, "You're a damn Nazi! Get the hell out of here!" She jumped up and started screaming as two big men in brown shirts rushed down the aisle to the front of the auditorium to escort her out of the hall. Aunt Marion pulled away from the men and stomped out of the auditorium with her sisters not far behind.

When Aunt Marion reached the door, several reporters tried to talk to her, but in between her cussing and fuming, all they got were nasty remarks about those "damn Nazis." I don't think Mom or Aunt Ella fully realized what had happened, as they all went down to Plankinton Avenue to catch the Number 18 streetcar to go home.

That night, we had several calls from the *Milwaukee Journal* for Mom, and the next day the *Milwaukee Journal* had the story of the women who had disrupted the Christian rally. At that time, many people were unaware of the Nazi threat and how the recently organized youth bund camps (officially the German American Bund) were preparing loyalties for Adolf Hitler. Aunt Marion opened some eyes that night.

Tavern Talk

Every Saturday morning, Grandfather Wendland walked down to a local bar where a bunch of old men gathered to talk. All the men were from Germany, and they only spoke in their native language. They sat at the big round table in the back of the tavern drinking good German beer until someone came to pick them up and take them home. Several of the men supported Hitler and the Nazi party, and the more they drank, the more they made it known. To them, no one was as good as the Germans, and they thought Germany should take over Europe.

The talks went on week after week. The owner would tell them to keep it down. "People will talk, you know," he said, but the more the men drank, the louder they got. Finally, someone did report them.

Pa got a call from one of the neighbors. It seemed someone had been talking with those neighbors and asking questions about our family. Pa knew it must be someone from the government and went upstairs to talk with his dad. Grandfather Wendland just got nasty and told him to mind his own business. America was a free country, and he could say whatever he wanted.

In the meantime, that local tavern was being investigated, and there was talk it might have to close because it was hosting "Nazi club meetings."

We were told not to speak German at any time, and if anyone asked about Grandfather Wendland, we were to say he was just an old man who said dumb things. Little did we know that the army would soon be visiting our home.

The Beginning of the War

One Sunday after church, we planned to have dinner with Aunt Rosa and Uncle Stan in Milwaukee. Aunt Rosa was Pa's sister, and she was a fantastic singer, as all in the family were, and often sang on the radio. She had only been married to Uncle Stan for a few years, as her first husband died in a train accident. We were right in the middle of dinner when someone pounded on the door. Aunt Rosa lived in a large apartment building where Uncle Stan was the manager. The pounding came from the next-door neighbor who was shouting that we were at war. He told us to turn on our radio and then ran down the hall to spread the news.

"We interrupt this program for a special announcement," we heard. The radio air went dead for about ten seconds, and then a newsman came on and said, "The Japanese have attacked Pearl Harbor." One of the kids from church, Gerald Wyatt—Doug's brother—was stationed there and had just sent a letter to the congregation about how beautiful it was in Hawaii. Within hours, the newspapers had a special out with the story. On December 7, the Japanese had attacked our naval base at Pearl Harbor. I was only eight years old, but I knew that was really bad.

Soon, many Japanese-Americans and German-Americans were picked up and sent to internment camps across the U.S. The Bund camps were raided all over the country, and anyone who belonged to one of the camps was investigated by the FBI. Several kids from my school and their families had reportedly moved to Texas or California, but in reality, they were arrested and sent to the internment camps. I had a friend who lived in New Berlin just a few miles from our house. His neighbors ran German Bund meetings in their house and wore brown shirts like storm troopers. All the members were sent to the internment camps along with their party members.

My cousin Richie had just joined the American Army and would be sent overseas. Two weeks after the attack, Richie came to visit Pa and told him how they were trained with wooden play guns and jeeps that had attached to them large pictures painted onto plywood to make them look like enemy tanks. Several months after he was deployed, Richie was killed in the war.

German Prisoners

Mikey and I spent most of our time playing in the woods. In the spring, all the flowers came out and covered the woods like a blanket. We often picked flowers on the way to school and gave them to our teachers or picked a bouquet on the way home. We often dug out the violets and put them in one-quart berry boxes to sell in town for three cents each. We picked wild berries in the woods every summer, nuts in the fall, and cut down trees for firewood through the winter. The woods were our playground, too, where we played war games in the summer and fall and rode our sleds down the winding path to 88th Street in the winter. It was the pathway to school, church, and the grocery store, and it ran right through our property.

One late fall day, Mikey and I were walking home from school. It was a perfect time to climb the "trick tree"—that was the tallest and straightest tree in the entire woods. Mikey climbed up first. It was easy because the branches were close to each other, and we could reach up and grab a branch and then reach up and grab another until we got to the very top. It was just like climbing the monkey bars. Sometimes we would rock back and forth at the top of the tree and sway like we were on a swing set.

Just then, Mikey called me up higher in the tree and pointed out two men going into a vacant garage in the woods. They looked like they were wearing work coveralls. Many of our friends lived in garages or dugouts, but no one we knew lived in this garage. The owners had built it several years ago, but then they lost their money and couldn't afford to build a house. This place was all locked up, and nobody was supposed to be in there. Once in a while, some older kids would bust the lock and use the place for smoking, but not too often.

We looked in the garage and saw three men in jumpsuits sitting on boxes in the corner. They spoke to each other in German, but too quietly for me to understand what they were saying. I spoke and understood a little German because Grandfather Wendland sometimes spoke in German. He had told me that Germans were the master race, whatever that was. We were not allowed to speak German in public, though, or tell anyone we were German since the war had started. We were told to tell everyone that we were Welsh. They forgot to tell us we were part Jewish, too.

Every day, we stopped at the garage on the way home from school and looked through the knot hole to see if the men were still there. One day, when we were all eating dinner, my parents talked about the German prisoners of war working at the state fairgrounds because it was too crowded at Billy Mitchell Airport in Milwaukee, another prisoner-of-war site. The United States had German prisoner-of-war camps throughout the country, and a number were in Wisconsin, including the one at the Milwaukee Airport, Billy Mitchell Field. It had high fences around the barracks and high towers surrounding the complex. We drove by it one day just to see what it looked like. Pa stopped the car for a minute while we watched the prisoners walking inside the fence. A jeep came toward us and pulled in front of our car.

Three soldiers came out of the jeep with rifles and came to us, two on one side and one on the other. Once they saw kids in the back seat, they were very nice but told us we couldn't stop in front of the camp.

Once Mikey heard my parents talk about the prisoners. He told them that we had seen three men going into the vacant garage. Pa thought they might be hobos looking for a place to stay because the nights were getting colder. The garage wasn't far from the hobo camp, and all they had for shelters there were makeshift wood covers. Since the war had started, though, we saw very few hobos, and most of them were old. But we didn't say anything else about the men. We seldom talked at the table unless asked a question.

Children just listened to the adults.

It was about 2 a.m. when we heard loud noises in the driveway and the yard. We looked out of the window to see our house surrounded by the U.S. Army. Dozens of soldiers with rifles and other weapons were running out of the woods. Pa went to the front door, and they shouted to him to get back into the house.

A few minutes later, an officer pounded on the door and asked who was in the house and if anyone else was staying there. He pushed open the door and looked at us standing in the living room in our pajamas. He wanted to know who lived upstairs and told us no one could leave the house.

Most of the soldiers worked their way out of the woods and went through our garage, outhouse, and chicken coop. Several armed soldiers stayed back to watch us and the house. From time to time we heard gunshots and saw soldiers running from the chicken coop out to the woods. Then there was more gunfire, and several of the jeeps and trucks took off, but the guards stayed.

About thirty minutes later, the same officer came back to the house and wanted to ask us some questions. Did we know that there were enemy soldiers living in the woods? Then Pa took Mikey seriously and told the officer that we kids had seen three men breaking into the old garage, but he and Mom hadn't paid much attention to us at the time. Then the officer asked Pa if he had any contact with these men or knew they were there. At this point, I think Pa was concerned. Both our grandpas were from Germany, and Grandfather Wendland was a very outspoken supporter of Adolf Hitler and had no problem telling the neighbors (and the world if it would listen) what he thought. With several families being sent to retention centers and with the Bund camp found in Waukesha County, the Army was checking everybody out. Pa explained that his father and stepmother lived upstairs and were eighty years old.

That was the only time we were questioned, but I'm sure the FBI did some research on our family.

Living in the War

I had just come in from doing the chores. We had very few chickens by this time, but they still had to be taken care of. Spring was here, and we started to clean up the berry bushes and cultivate between the rows. The first thing I did when I was in the house was have a cup of coffee. I was ten years old but had been drinking coffee (and wine, although only when I said I had a cough) since I was about five.

I grabbed the sugar bowl and stirred two teaspoons of sugar into my coffee. My cousin, Shirley, who was over for breakfast, went ballistic. Shirley was Evelyn's age. "How dare you put sugar in your coffee? Our food stamps only allow us one pound of sugar every two months, and you put it in your coffee!" I had never seen Shirley this mad. They were living free in our house, but we all shared the stamps. I have never forgotten her outburst and never, never put sugar in my coffee again.

We had very few stamps for meat or other basic food essentials because of the war. Anyone caught cheating on the stamps was put in jail. It was like hating the flag! We all got sick of killing and eating our own chickens, plus we were running out of chickens. Pa decided to solve the meat problem. He bought three little pigs. Then he built a shed and fenced in an area for them to run and wallow in the mud. We named them Rufus, Peewee, and Peanuts. They were friendly pigs, and after they were full-sized, Mikey and I rode on their backs.

In the fall, the first one was butchered, and all the meat was smoked and hung in the attic. Pa even made the pork into sausage links for sandwiches. Each year we ate off one pig, and we were the richest people I knew. What a feast, but not good for the pigs.

War Rationing

We loved to go fishing, but one of our biggest problems was not having enough ration stamps for gas with the war raging. Pa never drove the car to work; he always took the bus. Mom didn't drive, so we used very little gas. But we were allowed so little that we didn't have enough to drive out of town to fish. Pa said that someday companies would make gas out of corn, and the cobs would be used to heat stoves. When my parents were first married, that's what they used for heat. Pa was far ahead of his time.

Pa looked at a number of supplements for gas and found an ingredient called white gas that was used for stoves. He couldn't see why we couldn't mix white gas with gasoline. So, he started mixing the two gases using varying combinations. He finally developed a formula that worked in the car and bought white gas and stored it in ten-gallon cans. He could buy as much white gas as he wanted and then just mixed it with the gasoline. We went fishing all summer long for the next three years. If Pa had his way, he would have lived on a lake. Every weekend in June, we went to Mud Lake or fished off the pier at Port Washington.

We picked and sold berries during the week and took care of the chickens and the pigs until the bank sold the property that we used to raise produce and chickens. The bank started to build two-story apartments. In fact, the old chicken coop was used for the second level of one of the new buildings. Because of the war, the builders put up the first floor of the building in blocks and then lifted the second floor of the chicken coop, which had been a house, on top of the blocks to complete the house.

War Games

Everyone was in position, waiting. After hours of cutting shrubs to build hiding places and getting the handguns ready for action, we waited. Mikey was to be on one side and Vince on the other. Four of us waited behind trees. We had recruited as many neighborhood kids for the war as we could. The Walker kids would come storming up the winding sled hill path at any minute to attack our front lines.

This time, they had to play the Japanese. When we played war games the week before, we had to pretend to be the Japanese. Ever since the Great War started, we played war almost every day. Now we knew why the Japanese bought all the pig iron a few years before.

Every one of us owned a play rifle and helmet. This hill was our favorite place to play because it had a lot of undergrowth where we could hide. In the summer, we played Tarzan and swung from tree to tree with vine ropes. In the winter, this was the favorite sledding hill for miles around because of its winding path that dodged trees and stumps. As soon as the first snow came, we would start belly-flopping down the wooded hill from morning until night. It was most often below zero, but nobody seemed to worry about the weather. It was the only hill for several miles.

But for now, we had to be quiet. We could hear the Nelson kids coming up the sled hill, swarming like ants. They must have had twenty or more kids on their side. It was no wonder they always won every battle. Every time we played war with them, it ended up in a social disagreement. They never played dead after we shot them, so I felt obligated to knock them down. The fight would start again, and we would be in an all-out war.

What great fun.

Epidemic

A couple with a three-year-old girl named Millie moved in next door. Millie was a pretty little girl with black hair. She came over to our house every day. Pa worked in the yard with the berry plants during the daytime and then worked at Harley Davidson during second shift. When he had black topsoil and fertilizer, he would fill a wheelbarrow and push it to mulch the berries. Millie followed him back and forth as he worked. When he stopped to have his lunch (summer sausage or liver sausage), Millie and Pepper would sit and eat with him.

Pa loved the little girl as much as we all did, but Pa was special to Millie. She always called him "Granddaddy," a term used in the South since her parents were from Kentucky. One day, Millie came over from the house very excited because she was going back to Kentucky to visit her grandparents. She was such a happy girl.

A week after that, when Millie and her parents were scheduled to come home, Millie's dad called Pa and told him that Millie had died from polio. Pa walked to the front porch without saying a word and cried. It was the first time I saw my Pa cry. He didn't go to work that night; he just sat on the porch looking out the window. Three days later, Pa told us to pack our bags. By this time, the polio epidemic had gotten worse in the Milwaukee area, and children under sixteen were not allowed to leave their homes. This was the first time a whole city was quarantined. Every day, the paper would have a list of polio cases and a list of how many had died the day before.

We loaded everything in the car and headed out of town. When we asked where we were going, Pa said, "Someplace where you are safe." He had rented a cottage on Pewaukee Lake located about two doors down from Waukesha Beach, a small amusement park. Aunt Rosa, Shirley, and her daughter, Barbara, knew the owner of the cottage, who was out of town and wouldn't be back until the end of the year. The epidemic got worse in the big cities, but very few cases broke out in the country and none in areas close to us. When more cases were reported, Pa decided he wouldn't let us go back home until November. He worked all week and took care of the berry business and joined us on the weekends. It turned out to be a very fun summer.

Pewaukee Lake

Waukesha Beach attracted hundreds of tourists and residents every weekend, and it was right next door to our cottage. How good could it get? The cottage was a year-round house with four bedrooms, a large living room and kitchen, and a screened-in porch overlooking the lake. Aunt Rosa, Shirley, and Barbara were waiting for us when we drove up. Aunt Rosa had divorced and planned to move in with us that fall until they could find a house. Shirley had married Phil Green, who was in the Navy and stationed overseas at that point. I didn't know where Mikey and I would end up sleeping once everyone moved back into our house with us.

We met Walt Goodman, a friend of Aunt Rosa's, while at the cottage, and he visited us often. He had come to America in the 1920s and couldn't find a job. He picked up beer and soda bottles and sold them back to the breweries. It turned out to be so profitable for him, he built his own company out of it, with a large building as the headquarters where he bought and resold washed bottles. I guess he was a rich man. After the Prohibition, he started a wholesale liquor business in Milwaukee and owned several supper clubs around Wisconsin.

The first couple of weeks at the cottage we had a great time. Everyone got along well, and every weekend, Mikey and I practically lived at Waukesha Beach. For twenty-five cents, we could go into a huge building that housed nine different rides and slides and stay there all day. So we did.

Shirley was always teasing and spending time with Mikey and me, but her mood began to change. When the *Milwaukee Sentinel* was dropped off every morning, she pored over the stories about the war and the V2 bombers that Germany was using to bomb Great Britain. Britain couldn't seem to protect herself. She consistently talked about Cousin Richie, who was lost at sea when his ship was torpedoed. Several times we found her crying, but she wouldn't tell us why. Every time the mailman came, she refused to look through the letters. Her mood started to rub off on everyone in the family. None of us could figure out the root problem.

Then the worst happened. Shirley was called from the village that a telegram was waiting for her. She broke out crying, and Walt Goodman said he would pick it up for her or drive her into the village. Everyone was gloomy as Shirley and Walt drove away.

She was gone about twenty minutes. The grownups sat idly, waiting, and growing anxious. Walt's car finally pulled up into the driveway, and Shirley jumped out before it had even stopped. "He's okay! Phil's okay!" she cried. Everyone started laughing and shrieking and hugging, but Mikey and I didn't have a clue what was going on. Phil was back in Florida. He had just returned from a mission in Great Britain, but his ship was safe. Shirley knew he was supposed to be stationed in Great Britain, but she hadn't heard from him in two months.

It was the first time I realized how horrible the war was. Before that, it was just an event happening somewhere far away to someone else. But here it was, touching my life in a number of ways I hadn't even realized.

When we got back home at the end of the summer, Phil was on leave, so Mikey and I slept on the porch floor. I'm glad no one else moved in, or we would have been stationed to sleep in the chicken coop.

My Appendix

In the fall of 1942, Aunt Rosa, Shirley, and Barb moved in with us. Pa worked second shift, and Mom worked for the YWCA. Shirley's husband, Phil, was on leave from the Navy and used Walt Goodman's delivery truck for transportation until he went back.

No one was home when I doubled up with pain. My right side felt like it was bursting, and I started throwing up. Phil found me and after one look, picked me up, threw me into the back of the delivery truck, and headed to the hospital. The truck was full of liquor and beer and empty bottles. He drove the truck for the Midwest Liquor Company, which Walt Goodman owned.

Phil drove so fast some of the bottles of beer juggled all around me, and I rolled side to side as he turned corners. One of the beer bottles broke on me and soaked me in beer. When we got to the hospital, Phil didn't wait for a gurney. He just picked me up in his arms and ran me into the hospital. I was rushed into surgery for a burst appendix, which I supposed was kind of bad. I was lucky that Phil had found me, and the hospital had caught it in time because it could have been fatal.

I stayed in the hospital for a week, and when I came home, Phil had gone back to the Navy, and Walt Goodman had moved in with us. The house was getting crowded, and I lived in the living room on a couch. My aunt and her family lived with us for about two years before Walt bought a place on Sherman Boulevard, and they all moved out. I finally got a bed of my own. After that, Mikey lived with us, and my cousin Jack, Uncle George's son, who was six years older, moved in for a year. But I kept my bed.

Between Cars

Every Saturday, Mikey and I would finish our chores, and then Pa would give us two bits to go to the movies. By this time, the cost had gone up to ten cents or even twelve cents for some theaters—all that for just three movies, two ten-minute shorts, one twenty-minute serial, and five cartoons. The movies started at noon and only lasted until 4:30 p.m. What a rip-off!

We often left the house at 11:00 a.m. and walked through the fairgrounds and down Greenfield Avenue to the Allis or Capitol theaters. Sometimes we would go to the Paradise Theater, but it always cost us twelve cents, and the workers at the theater complained because we brought in popcorn we had bought at the sweet shop.

One Saturday, we stopped at Freeze's Candy Store and bought a taffy apple covered in caramel and then headed to the show. The westbound Number 18 streetcar was coming, so I grabbed Mikey and ran fast to beat the car to get across the street to the movie. We jumped in front of the train just as the eastbound had taken off. Somehow, we ended up between the two trains with less than a foot's clearance between the two cars. I don't think either engineer knew we were stuck in between the trains. We were only two small kids, but that streetcar was right against our faces. This was the first and only time Mikey didn't panic. We were both too frightened to move. We weren't touched by the cars, but we stood looking into the window, nose-to-nose with passengers who just gasped at us. One woman started screaming, but we couldn't even think about what she was saying. One streetcar kept going, but the second one stopped because of the woman screaming.

When it was clear, we stood still, catching our breaths. One car's conductor ran out, but we thought we would get in trouble and ran in line with all the kids getting into the theater. In the crowd, the conductor didn't know who we were.

Somebody is Missing

After Mikey moved in, we spent every day together. Between May and September, we went to the state fairgrounds every night because of the midway. The rides started at about 7:00 p.m., but they would allow kids to ride them free until opening. The only rides we never went on were the rollercoaster and the Loop o' Planes. But we often searched for money under the rollercoaster because some people lost change during the ride's ascent or loops. Mikey went on the Loop o' Planes once, but he threw up after that.

The Moat was a boring ride located on the midway, but a lot of the kids liked it because they could play tricks on the operator. The Moat was a boat that meandered through a small building with scary monsters that jumped out at passengers. In reality, it was so slow, it became more of a Lover's Lane ride. Couples would take the ride to kiss and make out. When passengers got onto the boats, they were instructed to keep their hands inside the boats and not to stand up. But sometimes, kids still jumped out of the boats and waited to hop into the next one that drove through.

Four kids could ride in each boat. Halfway through the ride, one kid would climb off and sit on the sidewalk used by the operator if there was trouble. When the boat got to the end of the ride, only three kids would still be riding. The operator didn't seem to know how many were in the boat to start with. Then the next boat that had only two kids when it started now held a third kid—the one from the earlier boat. In that case, the operator remembered that the boat had only two kids. He questioned the kids, but they insisted they had started with three. The operator never caught on, or so we thought.

One day, the kids made their first mistake. The Moat had a new operator who must have been warned about their tricks. When traffic was slow, the operator would let an empty boat go through to keep the ride going. All the boats were connected, and if you fully stopped one boat, they all stopped.

Three local kids got into one boat. They didn't know the next boat would be empty. They thought a couple other kids would be in it. When the empty boat came, one of the kids jumped in, but he rode that one all alone. When he came out of the ride, the operator caught him. He held the boy until the fair police took him to the station. I don't know what happened to him, but Mikey and I didn't try to play that trick.

It was a pretty great life. Just two little kids going to the fairgrounds every night and riding for nothing, and parents never worrying about us because we always came home on time and never caused any trouble. ☆☆

Chapter Ten | 1945–1947
More Adventures

Haunted Tent

After the war, everyone could buy war surplus very inexpensively at stores. Kids bought Army field jackets or boots as everyday wear. We really looked grown up in those jackets. Pa bought us an Army tent meant to sleep two. It was only six feet long and four feet high. We had two Army cots that were the perfect size for the tent. Mikey and I spent much of the summer sleeping in our tent. It was our getaway. We used to set up the tent on any spot on the farm or even in the woods. The tent had two poles at each end with a cross pole supporting the top. The sides were made of a fabric wall with extended ropes on each corner to give it stability.

We spent one month in Port Washington at Evelyn and Glenn's house in the country. It was a great location, just a mile from the city of Port Washington and a half-mile from Lake Michigan. We made our breakfast and then went to the lake for a swim. There was also a mud pond at Port that we hung out at for the day.

When we came back home in September for school, we set up the tent in the back of the farm in the old apple orchard and decided to spend a night in it. We had a lantern inside and one hanging from a nearby tree. Mikey and I were both on our cots in the night when all at once the tent began to shake. It got worse and worse, almost like we were in a tornado, but there wasn't even the slightest breeze. Mikey thought I was shaking the end poles, but I wasn't near them. The swaying got worse, so we took turns jumping out of the tent to see if anybody was around. No one was there. We never touched the poles, and every time we got into the tent, it shook worse.

The next day I called my cousin Denny to stay overnight and get his opinion on what was happening. The tent once again shook so hard that the top bent over. We moved the tent a short distance away and nothing happened. My friend Martin from school came over and claimed we were shaking it ourselves until we all walked over to the other side of the yard and it still shook.

I didn't believe in spirits and those sorts of things, but I could never explain this. We had heard that bootleggers had been buried on the farm by a mob, but we never knew for sure.

A Night to Remember

Uncle George and my cousins came over once a week. Uncle George was Mom's baby brother (ten years younger), and they were very close. When Mom and Pa owned a popcorn stand in West Allis, George was just a teenager and worked for them on weekends. During that time, he and Pa became best friends. The stand was located next to the Capitol Theater across from the Allis Theater. It was instant success, and my parents finally had some extra money. Mom wanted to use their savings from the stand to buy a new living room set since they still had the old couch from Grandma's house, and it was very worn out.

Pa and George were picking up supplies for the stand when they decided to stop and look at new cars. They found a dark green Essex almost brand new for only $400. The two of them tried out the car and found it had mohair seats and windshield wipers. It was a great car. Pa knew Mom wanted a new living room set, but he and George really liked this car. Then the salesman pointed out that they couldn't drive a sofa, but they could always sit in a car.

This made perfect sense to Pa and George. They bought the car and drove it down to the popcorn stand to show Mom. She took one look at the car and agreed that Pa was right: not only could a person sit in the car, but Pa could also sleep in it for the next three nights, she said.

One day, when I was twelve years old, Uncle George asked if I could babysit his kids for one night to earn a whole dollar. Little did I know that no one else wanted to babysit for him. He picked me up in the afternoon, and I played with the three kids until my aunt and uncle left. Joey was eight, Carolyn was six, and Jack was four years old. Once Uncle George and Aunt Elanor were gone, all hell broke loose. Both boys jumped from chair to chair, tearing up the house.

Eventually, Joey and Carolyn sat down and played a game with me, but Jack went off on his own. It took me several hours before I got them to bed at 11:00 p.m. I crawled up onto the couch and thanked God it was over. Then the worst happened.

One of the kids threw up all over the bunkbed and onto the floor. I was running to find a pail when the second kid threw up. I tried to get them to throw up in the pail, but Carolyn and Jack were too upset. The house didn't have indoor plumbing, so I grabbed all the towels I could find and started to clean up the floor. I took all the bedding off the beds and hung it on the clothesline.

The sickness lasted for about two hours before it finally stopped. By that time, every room in the house stunk as they had consistently missed the pail and finished up in the living room. At 5:00 a.m., I got both Jack and Carolyn back to bed. Joey tried to help, but he was too little and got tired of trying. I went back to the couch and heard Uncle George and Aunt Elanor singing and shouting as they came through the back door. They were so drunk they didn't look at the house or comment on the odor.

The kids got up at 8:30 a.m. and seemed to be much better, wanting French toast for breakfast. After 1:00 p.m., Uncle George woke up and was very nice—as he always was—and offered to take me home. No one could help what had happened, but I never, *never* babysat again. ✩

Chapter Eleven | Summers of 1945–1947
The Fair!

The Circus Train

Mikey and I jumped out of bed and ran down the stairs for breakfast. It seemed like forever before we could rush out the door, through the woods, and off to Spring Meadow Pond.

Everyone in the neighborhood spent hours at the pond located next to the railroad tracks. It used to be Hobo Junction before the war. Spring Meadow was, at one time, part of a large German park with beer gardens and dance halls, but when the railroad came through for the state fair park, most of the lake was filled in, leaving just a small deep pond. The springs were still there and were always full, but just smaller. Often, trash and tires thrown out of the railroad cars peppered the place, and grease that spilled from the trains spread through the water. We could fish or crab there, but we often used the pond for rafting or sailing our small boats with towlines. Anyone who swam there would sink in the mud and be covered with oil.

We waited at the side of the tracks for several hours for the big event: the circus train. Every year, the Al Ringling Circus would set up its tents at the fairgrounds, and all the kids in the area could help with the brief construction. Some of the older kids jumped on the freight cars and rode the train as it slowly moved across 84th Street and stopped at the north parking lot to unload the poles and canvases. Then the kids would follow the workers to the infield. I was too small to hop on the train, but Gene's friends always tried until one kid he knew slipped and tore half his arm off.

Once we reached the racetrack, the workers would work in pairs pounding in the corner stakes, hitting the huge spikes. One man would hit and lift his arm, and his partner would lower his huge hammer. Twenty teams of workers lifted their sledgehammers as if each one was playing a musical instrument. Then the huge canvas was stretched over the entire field, and a dozen teams of ten or more kids would lift the poles as straight as they could. Shortly after, the canvas blanket would be lifted to form a huge tent. It only took a few hours before all three canvas tents were standing and a small line of smaller game and concession stands were in place. After work was done, a hundred kids would line up for a free ticket to the circus.

The next day, the circus would open to thousands of people. There was no greater thrill than sitting on the bleachers in the huge tent and feeling that all of us kids were a part of it. Three days later, the shows ended, and the morning after they did, the entire circus would be gone to another city where another hundred kids would set up the tents. In just a few years, the tents would be gone forever, and this part of history would be forgotten. How lucky we were to be a part of it.

Walking on the Beams

Most of the kids in my neighborhood hung out at the fairgrounds all summer, and I loved being there. I knew every building inside and out. I had been over every square foot like it was my backyard. I dragged Mikey into most of my adventures, and we had a great time and didn't get killed—but we sure came close!

When the park was closed during the day, we would walk on the wooden log fences surrounding the picnic area near Greenfield Avenue. Then we would go down to the pig barns on 84th Street and play tag by running on the top of the stall dividers. The most fun we had was walking the beams in the old pavilion where livestock was judged during state fair week. The rafters were about thirty feet above the showing area and ten feet above the top of the bleachers. We used to play tag on the rafters for hours with kids from West Allis, Adler Street, or our neighborhood. Sometimes twenty kids played in the pavilion together, taking turns a few at a time running the beams, and I never heard of anyone falling off or getting hurt. Often it was so dark on the rafters that we all carried flashlights to follow the beams. With all those kids in one place, we made a lot of noise screaming and yelling at each other. The park police would get reports and search the building, and all the kids would lay very still on the one-foot-wide beams. The police would shine their lights between all the bleachers and around every corner, but they never looked up at the beams, and none of us ever got caught.

Mikey and I loved walking the beams or the wooden log fence, and we were very good at it. When we walked home, we followed the railroad track and would see if we could walk on the eight-inch steel rail that overlooked the traffic on 84th Street. Sometimes we would stand on the rail and watch the traffic cross underneath the tracks. There was only one track and only eight inches of clearance on either side of the track. The danger was if a train came. We didn't want to be standing on one of the rails when a train came and realize there wasn't enough room to stand between the train and the steel rail, so we always kept an eye open for a train, but they only came through three times a day.

But it did happen. We heard the train whistle as it turned around the bend coming toward the crossing. It was coming quickly and gave us only seconds to get off the rail and run down the tracks to the slope. We both panicked and froze—not a good thing to do at the time. We jumped off the rail and ran for the big embankment. The train whistle screamed at us, and the brakes screeched, and we knew we wouldn't make it to the end of the overpass in time.

Mikey was screaming, but I couldn't hear anything over the sound of the train. The steel rail was about two feet high, so I ran behind Mikey, forced him to the side rail, and pushed him over the top. He went head-first, like a baby bird taking off from its nest for the first time. In a second, I followed him over the rail, with my feet up against my chest, and stretched out as I cleared the rail. It was like diving off a diving board. I landed on the slope and rolled down to the sidewalk. At first my arm was twisted under my body, and it felt like it was broken. I couldn't get up for a few seconds because the shock to my head and body made me dizzy.

Oh my God, I thought. I had forgotten about Mikey. I may have pushed him over the top too early and into the traffic. I called and didn't see him, and I got really scared. The train must have come to a screeching stop because someone on the track asked if I was okay. Then I started to cry because I couldn't find Mikey. The guy said he saw the other kid lying near the roadside. I ran around the slope expecting to find Mikey in the middle of the road. I shouldn't have pushed him. What would his mother say when I told her I took him walking the steel rail above 84th Street and then pushed him over the top? "Hi, Aunt Marion. I killed your son."

Just then, I heard Mikey crying. He was lying on the inside of the slope just a few feet away from the overpass's supporting columns. He had just missed the concrete, but his face was pretty scratched up from landing on it and the top of his body. He wasn't seriously hurt, though.

That day, we learned not to stand in the middle of the track when waiting for a train. We learned to stick to the wooden beams thirty feet above the ground.

Fair Park

Every summer, I looked forward to going to the fairgrounds because I spent the whole summer on the midway. Every evening and all day on Saturdays and Sundays, the midway was open for rides and concessions. I would run down to the park before they opened to talk to the carnival workers who ran the rides, and often I would get free rides just for running errands or watching the rides when the workers had to go the washroom.

When state fair week started, they charged admission to get in. Most of us kids didn't have any money, so we had to find creative ways to get in for free. We would try any way we could to sneak in. We went under the fence and over the fence and through the fence. On Family Day, Mikey and I would wait until a large family went through the gate, and then we would follow them in like we were part of their family. For several years, we could get into the park before it opened if we carried a gallon milk bottle and said we were buying milk from one of the farmers showing cattle. We'd carry the empty bottle in, bury it in a straw pile, and wait for the park to open. When they caught on to us, we had to find a new way.

The next summer, the fair crew let kids come in early to pick up empty coke bottles. Coke was five cents for an eight-ounce bottle of soda and a deposit of two cents a bottle. They gave kids ten cents for a case of twenty-four bottles and allowed the kids to stay for the fair when it opened. Mikey and I did this for a day and only made ten to twenty cents each. There were too many kids, and we had to fight all of them to claim a bottle. So, we decided to go into business for ourselves. We worked on the roadways nearest the outside fence. When we found a bottle, we threw it over the fence into the ditch. You couldn't break a Coke bottle if you hit it with a hammer.

We would turn in one case of bottles to collect a dime and stay for the fair. When we left, we collected our hidden bottles and took them to the grocery store across the street for forty-eight cents a case. We picked more bottles when we worked for ourselves and made fifty cents each day. After two days, fair workers caught on to us—or somebody squealed—and we were thrown out of the park. That's when we came up with a different foolproof way to sneak in!

A New Idea

Mikey and I got up early, had a big breakfast, and got ready to go to the state fair. The state fair was the biggest event of the year, and we never wanted to miss a day. We packed up a couple of sandwiches, chips, flashlights, and old tennis shoes. The weather was nice and warm with evening showers expected. We only lived three blocks from the fair, so we reached the entrance in ten minutes.

It cost twenty-five cents to get into the fair, but that was too much for us. All the neighborhood kids climbed the fence to get in, but barbed wire was put up at the top of the fence after we were caught. Then we started going down to Greenfield Avenue through Honey Creek, but that was fenced off. Finally, we tried walking around the fence line looking for cuts in the fence or places we could burrow under.

One day, I was scoping out the fence when I found an opening from the drainage ditch. A culvert pipe opened up into a four-foot-high tunnel that ran under the entire fairground from 84th Street five blocks to the racetrack's infield before it drained into Honey Creek and 76th Street. It was about a half-mile underground and connected with all the surface water from the roadways in the fair. The opening was hidden from the road because of tall grass and a number of bushes.

The first time we went into the tunnel, we didn't know how far it went. We had to walk in a few inches of water and chased a few rats as we stumbled through. After about twenty minutes, we came out in the racetrack. We started using this entrance for many of the special events at the grandstand. In those days, the Green Bay Packers played their home games at the park. We would take our flashlights and lunches and go under the fair and come up inside the grandstand. We snuck into the bleachers at the end zone and watched the game until halftime. The stands were usually empty at halftime because nobody went to the games so we would move up to the thirty- or forty-yard line for the second half. After the games, the players in uniform went up and down the stands and greeted the fans.

We climbed down into the ditch and checked to see if anyone was watching. It surprised me that no one had found this way before, but it was well hidden. The clouds were moving in early, and it looked like we could get an early shower, but that wasn't in the forecast. We had used this method for the last two years and didn't see any other kids in there, nor did we tell any of our friends about our special entrance. One time we had gotten caught going to the auto races in the fall. When we came out of the sewer into Honey Creek, the revealing stand was right above us, and someone saw us coming through. He said, "Damn you, kids! Go back where you came from!" We ran back through like our lives depended on it. We thought the cops would be waiting on the other end, but no one was there.

We checked to see if we had everything: two flashlights, lunch, and tennis shoes in case there was water in the sewer. Tennis shoes would dry quickly. We ducked down and pushed the bushes aside, and there was our secret entrance. In fifteen or twenty minutes we would be on the track and just through the grandstand into the park. I heard thunder as we entered the cave, but it wasn't raining. We turned on the flashlights and started splashing through a few inches of water. The one thing that was unusual this time was that there weren't any rats to greet us. We weren't afraid of rats. Every spring, Pa would break up the rats' nest under the outhouse, and the rats would scatter all over the yard. Pepper loved to catch rats, and so did we. Each kid would arm himself with a baseball bat, and we chased them around, trying to hit them with our bats. I don't think I ever hit any, but it was a great sport.

We had been wading for about five minutes and had gotten just past the first road to the fair. There was a large grate in the middle of each road to let in some light and air. I could hear the thunder, but I never gave it a thought, other than the fact that we should have brought jackets. As we got further into the sewer drain, I noticed there was more water than usual.

Then I heard a loud roar that didn't sound like thunder. The water was getting deeper and now over the tops of our shoes. The roar got louder and louder, and the water rose faster and faster. I had never been in the drain when this happened; now I was getting concerned. The noise was so strong that I could hardly hear Mikey talking. Finally, it hit me—there was a big storm outside, and all the water from the sewer pipes and street storm sewers was emptying into the tunnel and running toward us.

We didn't realize we had been walking down a gradual decline. We had to get back to the entrance. Mom had always read stories in the newspaper about kids who died in the storm ditches. I had always wondered who could be so dumb as to fall into a ditch of flowing water? We turned around, and by then, the water was almost up to our knees and knocking us over. Mikey screamed and kept stopping, but I just kept hitting him to go forward. We had to get past the first storm sewer from the road, but I didn't know if we could make it. Mikey couldn't go much faster and was easily knocked over by the force of the water. I pulled him up, but he lost his flashlight, and mine wasn't much help.

We tried to lean up against the wall to hold our balance. We were crawling along the wall as if it would protect us from drowning. We got to the last storm sewer where the water was coming through the road grate in one solid wall. Now I wished I could swim. I thought back to when I fell off the pier at Uncle John's cottage and was terrified. Mikey was afraid to walk through the wall of storm water, but I punched him forward so I could get through. As we got four or five feet away from the floodwater, the water seemed to lessen, and it was easier to walk. The water had dropped below our knees, and we could see the entrance of the drain. We reached 84th Street and crawled up over the drainage ditch. It was raining hard, but we didn't notice. We must have laid on the ground for several minutes. Mikey was still crying, and we both couldn't talk.

We staggered to our feet. Our legs felt like lead weights as we wobbled across 84th Street and headed home. When we walked in the door, Mom saw us and told us to get into dry clothes. We never told her what happened because we would have gotten a lecture. We were so tired we didn't even talk about it.

The next day we went to the fair and paid the twenty-five cents. That evening, when we got home, Mom read in the *Milwaukee Journal* about some kid who had drowned in a storm sewer in a flash flood. "Boy," I told Mom, "was he ever stupid."

A Little Cash

We were always looking for ways to make extra money for the fair. Many of the owners of houses located across from the park and up to a block away allowed cars to park on their lawns for thirty-five cents to fifty cents a day. Hundreds of fairgoers parked in private parking lots. We were located four blocks from the park entrance, but we had a large vacant lot next to the house that would be perfect for parking.

Gene and I went down to 84th Street with a small sign: "Parking–25 Cents." This was the best price in the neighborhood. Cars would stop, and we would tell them we were located just a little way down the road. We would jump on the car's running board and hang onto the windows and start directing them four blocks down to the farm where the parking was.

After several blocks, the drivers would stop and ask us where we were going. "Just a little further," we would say. After another block, they would start to get mad. Sometimes they turned their cars around with us still clinging to the windows and trying not to fly off the running boards. We tried it for a whole day and never parked a car.

Skee Ball and Little Mack

Gene spent many weekends at the fairgrounds with his friends. It was the hangout for the neighborhood. If you wanted to meet girls, you went to the fairgrounds with its popular midway. Gene spent so much time there, he ended up playing Skee-Ball for hours and got very good at it. He came home with so many big gifts he had won. Sometimes, he would win a stuffed animal for a girl who was watching him play. When you played the games as much as we did, you knew which ones you could beat, and he beat the Skee-Ball game.

Sometimes I went down to watch him play. He had developed a method of rolling the ball up against the side of the alley so it would bounce into the fifty-point hole. You could get ten to fifty points for each ball. You were given nine balls, so a perfect game was 450 points. Gene could get a perfect game almost every time. For 450 points, you got 75 tickets for gift items, and the game only cost a nickel. For 75 tickets, you could win a toaster that originally cost $2.00 or a six-piece glass set worth $1.50. You could save up for and win anything from throw rugs to golf clubs.

Gene won a lot of neat items but never made a career of playing and breaking the game, but I did! I'd go down every day and practice bowling the ball the way Gene did. It took me a while to master the game, but after several weeks, I could score a 450 nine out of ten times. Every night, I would go down to the building that had Skee-Ball and play about twenty games. Skee-Ball was the biggest game they had in the park.

There were eighteen alleys, and most were typically full. Nobody seemed to win more than a few tokens, and they just wasted their money, but then again, it was just for fun. For me, it was a business.

One night, I started to play when two big men came over to watch me. After I finished my game, they told me I wasn't allowed to come into that building again. I didn't know what to do, and I was scared. I didn't stay in the park but went right home and told my brother. He said he would go in with me, and they couldn't stop me from playing.

The next day, Gene went in with me, and we both started playing. Gene was just as good as I was, and both of us were winning 450 points. The two men came in but never questioned us. One guy stayed, and every time I finished a game, they closed that alley. I moved on to another alley, and the same thing happened. They closed down the game, and the cashier closed up. Everyone had to leave, and they turned off the lights and pulled a large folding door across the front of the building. I could not believe they had closed. The next day, I came to the park, went to the Skee-Ball building, played a couple of games, and they closed again.

This happened for three days, and finally, the two big men came back. "Little Mack wants to see you, kid." I had never heard about Little Mack before, but I finished the game and followed the two big guys. I don't think this was too smart, but for some reason, I followed them across the field to the administration building. I walked through a dimly lit hallway to the back of the building. A nasty little man sat behind a desk with a snarl on his face, like it was supposed to be a smile. "So, you're Eddie," he said. "You're a pain in the ass, kid. You're costing me a lot of money."

He stood up and was five feet tall. He wore a dark shirt and a black sports coat. He reminded me of the Penguin character from Batman. "You're killing my business, kid. So, what are we going to do about it?" He asked me if I was as good at playing the other games at the fair. I could beat some of the games, but even if I won, it didn't pay. Skee-Ball had the best prizes. The basketball game had a smaller hoop and was hard to beat. The game where you shot down the dolls had weights on the bottom, so you had to hit the very bottom of the doll to push it off the shelf. Yeah, I could beat most of the games, but I had been playing them for the last five years. I had even worked with the carnie men who told me the tricks, but I didn't tell that to Little Mack.

So Little Mack hired me as a shell for fifty cents an hour, free rides, and a special price on concession food. Every day after school and on weekends, I played games and won prizes to attract customers to the games. I did this for the rest of the summer. I don't think I ever told my parents exactly what I did at the park. I just told them that I was hired to help the owner of the concessions.

Many years later, I helped a city hire a carnival for their three community events. I met with the carnie and tried to negotiate but had a hard time dealing with them until I told them I wanted a clean operation—no weights in the dolls, no small hoops, and no shorting the customers on the balls in Skee-Ball. And when I told them I had worked for a carnie, and Little Mack was my boss, I got new respect. It takes one to know one. ☆☆

Chapter Twelve | 1947
The End of Childhood

The Girl with the Kinky Hair

Every other weekend, Mikey would stay with his mother, and I would stay at my cousin Denny's house. Denny was more like a brother to me than my brother and even closer to me than Mikey. We always had fun together and never fought. But then, Denny was always so easygoing.

One day, Aunt Ella sent us to the corner store on 10th Street. Every neighborhood had a corner grocery, and there must have been a hundred of them just in Milwaukee. One reason for the abundance of stores was that people could put their food bills on charge until payday.

We ran down to the store two blocks from the house and stood in line. I saw a little girl ahead of us who had shiny black hair all knotted up in curls that clung to her head. For some reason, I kept staring at her. Denny didn't notice, but I couldn't take my eyes off that girl. She glanced at me like she knew I was staring at her. Sometimes a person can feel eyes on them. I don't know why. She was uncomfortable, but I couldn't stop looking at this girl like I knew her and knew her well.

Denny was buying the sugar, and I had the greatest urge to talk to this girl. When we walked out of the store, I asked Denny if he had noticed the little girl or knew who she was. But he hadn't paid any attention.

I thought about her all night. I never forgot seeing her, and six years later, I actually met her. And after that, I married her.

Another Attack

It had been eight years since I had rheumatic fever, and over the previous four years, I seemed to get better. I ran and played as much as anybody. I still had a heart murmur, but nothing serious.

Pa and I went down to the feed store to buy our spring seed and grain for the chickens. I helped Pa load the trailer, and we headed out to the riding stables to visit Mr. Camp. He owned the horse farm, and his son, Kenny, had been a good friend of mine. Sometimes I would go to the farm by myself and spend the afternoon riding and playing with Kenny. It was only a half-mile from our house, and I could ride the horses for nothing. A month after my last visit, Kenny was thrown from a horse and broke his neck. He died within a few hours. Kenny had been an excellent rider, so I don't know what happened. His father's heart was broken. Kenny had been his pride and his life.

Pa stood talking with Mr. Camp. I started to get dizzy and had pain in my chest. I couldn't seem to get any air to my lungs. I passed out in the driveway, and Pa put me in the car and rushed me to the nearest hospital. When I woke up, I had trouble breathing. Our doctor was called and arrived at the hospital within a few minutes. He was my new doctor and best we could get. I had several tests taken and spent a few days in the hospital before I was sent home to rest. The treatment for my heart murmur when I was four had been to refrain from running and playing hard and to sit as much as possible. Dr. Short, however, wanted me to treat my heart like a muscle: build it up, walk a lot, and start running as soon as I was well enough. Exercising the heart would strengthen the muscle. Mom was not happy with this doctor or his treatment method, but Pa felt he was right. Time has proven that he was right, and he was a great doctor.

Baseball Games and Basketball Fights

Our neighborhood baseball team was made up of our street kids and the four Shanahan girls who lived across the field from me on Schlinger Avenue. The Shanahan girls were the best players, and we were lucky to have them. I had just turned thirteen, and every time Annie Shanahan ran the bases, she would fall on top of me. How did she get to be so clumsy? I mentioned it to Mom one day, and she just laughed and said that happened sometimes when a girl reached a certain age. I didn't think it was a bit funny. What was the joke?

We were ready to play the other streets, and we had some great games. Annie was our best player and never fell on anyone else when she ran the bases. We liked to play the Walker Street kids, but it ended up in a fight every time we did. They were still mad that I had beat up Charlie T., and I was still mad because they were always gunning for Mikey. We decided to play a nine-inning game, so we selected a lot on 84th Street. We got a kid from another neighborhood to umpire the game. Everything went well until the Walker players complained about a call. We argued for a while, and yes, it turned into a fight.

The punches started flying, and then someone hit Annie, and her Irish came out. She started swinging the baseball bat at several players and connected it with some of them and really hurt them. I don't know what they were complaining about. At least she wasn't falling on them. We grabbed our baseballs, gloves, and Annie's baseball bat, and ran like the dickens. That was the last game we ever had with the Walker Street kids. Two of their players ended up playing professional baseball. One played for the Milwaukee Braves. I think he was the one Annie hit with the bat.

Years later, I stopped in the old neighborhood to get a haircut from my old barber. A forty-year-old man came in and thought he knew me. He said his nickname was Pigs, and he was one of the Walker Street kids. He said, "I remember you because you used to beat me up all the time." I apologized and told him I didn't do that anymore. It's not a nice way to be remembered.

My last fight after the famous baseball game was out of the area. Mikey and I decided to go to West Allis Park to practice basketball. There were no places in town that had hoops, so we had to go to West Allis Park. Four kids older than us were playing full-court and wouldn't allow us to use one basket. We got into an argument, and before I knew what was happening, a kid got behind me, and the other kids pushed me over. Once I was on the ground, they taught me a lesson by giving me a black eye, bloody nose, and two loose teeth. Evidently, they had never heard of social disagreements or fair play.

I wasn't used to losing, but I had never fought anybody from out of town. This was my second real fight (the first being with Doug), and I had lost both. Of course, Mikey took off and didn't help me. My third and final real fight was coming home from Nathan Hale High School in December when I found my house surrounded by half of the Walker kids. Mikey had smarted off to somebody again and gotten them all riled up. I fought my way into the house and found Mikey with a few bruises he probably deserved. When I came back, the gang went home. It wasn't much of anything, but it was nice to fight with friends in a social disagreement.

Pa's Lesson

In the spring of 1941, the WPA extended the city sewer down McMyron Street past our farm. This meant we could finally get indoor plumbing. So that fall, Pa had the toilet installed, and we no longer had to run outside to the outhouse.

We removed the old outhouse and built a shed for the pigs. Shortly after, Mikey came to live with us, and Aunt Rosa, cousin Shirley, and her daughter moved in for almost three years.

In 1946, we had a big celebration for our new bathtub. For the first week, we had to take a number for whose turn it was to sit in the tub. I was a growing boy, and I didn't like taking a bath in the washtub in the kitchen, plus I no longer fit in it.

We had one problem we hadn't planned on, though. Our well was going dry. Our well was located under the house, which was common for homes built in the 1880s. Back then, builders would hand dig the well, then build the house on top of it. Our well was only twenty feet deep, and there was no way to dig it deeper under the house. We had to dig a new well.

Pa had a well digger come out, and the well digger felt we needed a well forty to fifty feet deep to hit enough water, but we couldn't afford it. So Pa decided to dig one himself. He bought a four-foot twist posthole digger and started digging. Everybody thought he was crazy, but of course no one told him that. Once he got down four feet, he screwed off the top of the pole and added an extension pipe and dug four more feet. Then he added four more feet, and then four more, and so on. Every night and on weekends he would dig down four more feet until he was pulling thirty feet of pipe out of the hole, but still he hadn't found any water. Sometimes he would hit rocks or heavy clay, and he worked for hours trying to break through with over thirty feet of piping. Finally, he had to have Gene help pull up the pipe and take off the extensions. Once they got the posthole digger to the top, they would have dug maybe three feet more. Then they had to put all the pipes on to lower it back into the hole. They added nine four-foot sections and lifted up forty-two feet of pipe.

One Saturday morning after working for several hours, Gene and Pa came in for a beer and lunch. Gene had been smarting off to

Pa for quite a while, even making remarks that he was stronger, so Pa should watch out. Gene always told me that Pa was an old man and had better not tell him what to do. I started to worry that Gene was going to start a fight with Pa someday and hurt him. Gene was always rude to both Mom and Pa. If Pa was at work and Gene didn't like what we were eating, Mom would give in and make him something else. Pa never knew what was going on. What had happened to eating whatever was placed in front of you?

Pa worked second shift and took the bus to work. Gene wasn't sixteen yet, but he wanted to use the car. He would argue with Mom to give him the keys until she was so upset that she would break down and cry. I tried to defend Mom, but I was much smaller than Gene, and he would just pound me up and take the car. Pa never knew.

One day, Pa went to work, and Gene demanded the keys to the car. Mom said "no," and it ended in a three-way fight. Gene threatened to run away if he didn't get the car, but Mom held her ground. Later, Gene stole the keys, and when Cousin Norman came over, they pushed the car out of the driveway and went to a dance at the high school. Norman was always very nice and didn't know what had happened. Mom realized that the car was gone and ran down the street to catch them. It was a terrible scene. Pa got home at about 11:00 p.m. and asked where the car was. Mom cried and chased me off to bed. She didn't want me to tell Pa what had really happened. I think Pa finally found out what was going on, and he was mad. Pa never got mad. He told Mom he was going to get the car back. Mom told Pa not to hit Gene, but I hoped he would. It was far overdue.

Pa had to take the 84th Street bus to get to the high school. He walked out onto the dance floor and asked Gene for the car keys. Pa had just come from work and had on a greasy shirt and pants. Gene was so shocked that he didn't say a word and handed over the keys. Then he said, "How am I going to get home and take my date home?" Pa told him to steal somebody else's car, and he didn't give a damn. When Pa came back, I could hear him and Mom talking for a long time. I couldn't hear what they were saying, but I think the cat was out of the bag.

After working on the well, we were all sitting down for lunch, and Gene kept poking at Pa and saying, "I can take you, old man."

Pa didn't like it, and I think he was just waiting for the right time. "Come on, Gene," Pa said. "Let's see how strong you are." Mom tried to smooth things over and tried to get both of them to sit down and eat. Gene kept pushing Pa and poking at him, and it was just too much. Pa got up from the table and walked into the living room. "Come on, Gene, let's see how tough you really are." Gene followed him into the living room with a smirk on his face. Mom started shrieking, "No, Herb, no!"

"Shut up, Rose, I have to do this," Pa retorted. "This has to stop." Pa had never said anything like that to Mom. Mom started crying, and I thought Gene was really going to hurt Pa. I didn't say a word, but I was afraid for Pa. Gene was young, and he was strong.

Pa just kept saying, "Okay, come on." Gene ran across the room and dove into Pa. Pa fell like a load of bricks. I don't think he expected Gene to hit him with such vengeance. Gene meant business. There was a vicious look of hate on his face. Mom kept crying with her hands on her face in disbelief. I started to say, "Don't hurt Pa." I saw Gene jump on Pa when he was still down on his back, trying to pin his arms down like he always did to me. Then he would always spit in my face.

Pa pushed Gene's arms back and grabbed him around the chest and threw him several feet away. They both jumped up, but Pa grabbed Gene around the waist and flipped him upside down. He swung him around as if he were weightless and rolled him across the floor. Pa quickly retrieved his new "toy" and twisted him up like a pretzel. He played with him like a cat plays with a mouse. He knew from the beginning it was no contest but wanted to play with him for a while. There was no fight. It was no match, and it became embarrassing to watch. No matter how rude and rotten Gene was to Pa, there was no sense in going on.

"Have you had enough, big man," Pa asked, "or do you need a little more?" Gene was terribly angry. He pulled himself up and stormed out of the door. Mom started to run after him, but Pa shouted, "No, Rose, let him go. He needed a lesson and he got one." Pa got up and tucked his shirt in, never even breaking a sweat. "Let's eat. Eddie, get me a beer."

We ate lunch in a very quiet kitchen. Mom sniffled through her sandwich. Pa kept looking out the window, waiting for Gene to return. After thirty to forty minutes, Gene came back inside, his hair still messy. He was wiping his hands on his pants like he was nervous. Neither Pa nor Gene spoke right away. Finally, Pa said, "C'mon, old man. Let's get back to the well." Gene reached a hand out and Pa took it, and they shook like adults. Pa even clapped Gene on the back a few times.

Two weeks later, they finished the well, and we had plenty of water. The plumber came and hooked up the pipes and put the pump in. He commented that in all his years of drilling wells, he had never heard of anyone digging a well with a four-foot posthole digger. He probably wouldn't hear of it again.

Jack Moves In

Life had been very hard to Uncle George. His wages were low, his wife had been ill on and off for several years, and now she was in the hospital and needed long-term care. They had three little kids and no one to take care of them while Uncle George was at work or at the hospital with Aunt Elanor. His best choice was to break up the family for a short time by sending each kid to live with a relative.

Carolyn, the middle daughter at eight years old, was sent to Chicago to live with Aunt Elizabeth, Elanor's sister. Aunt Elizabeth had a boy about the same age as Carolyn and was a kind and patient lady who just loved Carolyn and could spoil her. Joey was the oldest at eleven years old and refused to leave his father and was truly old enough to care for the house and himself and assist his father. Jack was sent to our home and needed a lot of love and tenderness after living with a sick mother and depressed father. He was six years old, and he couldn't handle those burdens at that age. When Uncle George came over with Jack, even I could see the sadness in this little boy's face.

After his father left, Jack disappeared into the three-car garage that was once our machine shed. We looked for him for twenty minutes, calling for him like one would in search of a pet who had been hurt or scolded. We finally found him buried under bales of straw. He never cried; he just looked sad, like no one would ever love him again.

Pa, who was always great with kids, picked him up and cradled him in his huge arms like a little puppy and hugged him closely. "Hey, partner," he soothed, "I missed you. I always wanted a little boy like you again. Let's go for a ride and get some ice cream. That always makes me feel better." The two of them got into the car and went to Thompkin's Ice Cream Store for a banana split, Pa's favorite dish, and came back about an hour later.

By that time, Jack was holding onto Pa's leg so he wouldn't run away, and Pa had him wrapped around his finger like he did with all the kids. When Jack went into first grade, he was the smartest kid they had ever had. And I do mean the smartest. He made a lot of friends, especially with the little girls who all loved his blonde curly hair—even at six years old.

Jack and our dog, Pepper, became fast friends and often chased rabbits in the woods together. Pepper caught them and carried them back to Jack. The rabbits may have been wet and shocked a little, but they weren't hurt, and Jack would wipe them off and return them to the woods.

In second grade, some older kids tried to beat Jack up because a girl liked him, but once he ran into the woods. No one could catch him. He was always finding new paths and hiding places under the bushes they couldn't get to. Jack stayed with us for about a year and left behind a lot of friends and a sad Pa but a better outlook on the future. He truly loved our happy home, and he always had a special place in his heart for Mom and Pa because of his visit.

Pa Opens a Restaurant

Over the years, my parents opened several businesses. They realized that factory and office workers had to drive to a local restaurant for lunch or bring a sandwich to work, so my parents decided to open a restaurant with a catering service to factories for lunch. This time Pa planned to quit his job and devote his time to the business. Mom and Pa found a location on 5th and Bruce Streets, three blocks from National Avenue. It was near the Valley and had a number of large factories nearby.

The neighborhood was a disaster. All the storefronts had been closed for many years, and the streets were deserted. All the buildings were falling down and infested with large sewer rats. Most of the buildings were full of old fixtures and dirt basements perfect for breeding new nests of rats. Why Pa picked this neighborhood, I'll never know, but he had always been right in the past.

Pa cleaned out the building by himself. He drew all the plans for the layout and design and started updating the wiring and plumbing. He put in a new linoleum floor over the plank wood boards and painted the interior and exterior of the building. He bought the counter, stools, stoves for cooking, and coolers, and built the rest of himself. It took him two months to complete.

Pa opened up a new restaurant called the Mighty Tasty Lunch. He ran off flyers and had them sent to all the local factories and to the local businesses in the area. We were busy from the first day that we opened. There was nothing else in the area, and that was why he opened there. We didn't start the catering service for several more months because we needed a panel truck and more equipment. I left school at 3:10 p.m., ran down to the bus stop, and transferred onto the Number 18 streetcar that ran down National Avenue. I got to work by 4:15 p.m. and washed dishes until 7 p.m. I scrubbed the floor, and then Mom and I would head home by 8:30 p.m. The next day we would do it all over again. Mom did some of the cooking, waited on tables, and ran the business. Pa never could quit his job completely, but he was there every day and then went to work. I worked until noon on Saturdays, and Pa would pay me $1.00 a week for my work.

I had never gotten a whole dollar at one time, but now I could go to one of the big theaters in downtown Milwaukee that charged twenty-five cents admission. The Dinky Train (a small streetcar lookalike) went down 6th Street over the Valley, but it cost five cents to ride, so I walked to save the money.

We had the restaurant for about two years, and then Pa sold the business to a catering company. We were glad to be out of business, but now we had a few dollars to fix the house and take vacations.

I'll See You in My Dreams

I went to Nathan Hale for my first year of high school. Even after being one of the best students at LaFollette School, I had to take review math and English classes because my little farm school was not the best place for education. My brother had graduated from Hale the year before. He was a great musician, and I was not. He was a troublemaker, and I was not. I just couldn't fill his shoes. The second year, I went to Central High where Aunt Evelyn had graduated as valedictorian. How would you like to follow that?

In the fall of my junior year, my parents decided to sell our home and move to West Allis. I was really hurt. Grandfather Wendland and Margaret had moved to a nursing home where Grandfather later died at the age of ninety-nine. Aunt Marion and Mikey rented the upper flat for the last two years before we sold the farm. Mikey and I no longer played with the same friends because he was still in grade school and still being chased by most of the neighborhood groups.

I cried when we moved, even though I was sixteen years old. I would lie awake at night thinking about how someday I would buy the old farm back. All the memories came back, and I still dream that I'm little Eddie running in the yard with my gander. I can hear Grandpa Phillips teasing me and see him sucking raw eggs. I can see the whole family sitting in the kitchen listening to the radio and trying to get warm near the stove. I even think about our first shower in the garage. The old dreams come back. ✩✩

About the Author

E dward "Eddie" Wendland was born in August 1933 and grew up in the suburbs of Milwaukee, Wisconsin, on a "city farm." He and his wife, Mary, were married one month shy of fifty years before passing away in 2003. They have five children and a number of grandchildren and great-grandchildren.

In 2014, Ed started to type the stories of his childhood on his typewriter, compiling them with the sole intent to gift them to his children and grandchildren as a Christmas present. Throughout the following six years, he continued to add stories, bringing in the help of an editor to arrange and rearrange until the book was in publishing format. Additionally, Ed has worked on finishing Mary's book, *Daisy in the Ashes*, polishing and editing, and eventually getting help from the same editor to write the final chapter.

Ed continues to fill his time typing stories for another book about his life and love with Mary called *With All My Heart*. ✩✩